A Contemplative Life

Essays and musings from the last of the baby boomers

by Charles F. Harrington

Copyright © 2020 Charles F. Harrington All rights reserved

No part of this publication may be reproduced, distributed, or transmitted in any form, or by any means, including photocopying, recording, or other electronic or mechanical methods, without the prior written permission of the publisher, except in the case of brief quotations embodied in reviews and certain other non-commercial uses permitted by copyright law.

This book is a memoir, it reflects the author's present recollections of experiences over time. Some names and characteristics may have been changed, some events have been compressed, and some dialogue has been recreated.

Cover and interior design; Charles Harrington

Cover Photo; Joel Trethaway, The Woodstock Academy.

ISBN: 9798577314972
Imprint: Independently published

Table of Contents;

Dedication
Introduction

Chapter One: The Irish, those who came before us.	13

Chapter Two: The wide-eyed wonder of our youth	27

Chapter Three: Coming of Age	53

Chapter Four: Sobriety	67

Chapter Five: The American Dream	79

Chapter Six: Loss and Sorrows	101

Chapter Seven: Hope for the future	119

Chapter eight: Love and Romance	143

Chapter Nine: Gratitude	159

Epilogue – The Plan	169

Dedication

It would be impossible for me to dedicate this work to just one person. My life which is chronicled herein, has been too powerfully influenced by too many. The list in no particular order is as follows;

My Parents of course, for all of the obvious reasons. They are my first heroes, my foundation and the source of all my strength and courage. I will forever be grateful to them for everything they gave to me. Along with my grandparents, aunts and uncles and all of the 'adults' from my childhood, the nuns and missionary priests, neighbors and friends and even babysitters, who all helped shape the world I came into. They, the ones who came before us, bequeathed to us so very much. Much that we sometimes have taken for granted or failed to fully appreciate. It was after all, all of them, that made all of us, possible.

My family and friends, of whom there never seems to have been any shortage of. I have been undeservedly blessed by these people, by their love and sincere kindness and patience. Too many to name, but not too many for me to remember.

My two best pals in the world, Scott and Mark, AND their children and grandchildren. These men for their relentless and devoted friendship that has spanned my entire life. Their children and grandchildren because they are not only their hope for the future, but all of ours as well. Just as my wonderful world was built by those that came before me, those courageous emigres of Ireland that arrived in America literally as children, and then set out to build a better life for their progeny, me among them.

So too are my friends Scott and Mark the ones that 'came before' their own progeny, and I am witness to all that they have done in a fashion no less remarkable than that of my ancestors. Their grandchildren will indeed benefit greatly from the sacrifices of these two fine men. That I believe, is how it is all supposed to work.

To my own children, Billy, Daniel, and Katherine. They have been my life's work and my eternal joy.

And finally, to my good friend Richard Telford. His insistence that I take on the role of 'The Stage Manager' in the incredible Thornton Wilder play 'Our Town', proved to be a life altering assignment. It was his imagination and perceptive foresight that thrust upon me that incredible and most challenging role. All for a fellow whose only previous stage experience was as Zacchaeus in a biblical play in the first grade at St. Mary's school. Rich was quite insistent that this was the role for me, and that I was the man for the role. He was, and could not have been, more correct. It was an incredible experience and I will remain forever grateful to him for the opportunity.

Introduction:

I do tend to go on a bit, ...

My lifelong pal Scotty's mom Lillian, who I have loved forever, was the first to describe me as having 'the gift of gab', and that was some fifty plus years ago.

I suppose my Irish heritage does play a significant part. I come from a long line of storytellers, was surrounded by them growing up, and it just kind of rubs off on you. I am also the middle child in a family of nine siblings, . . . four older brothers, and four younger sisters. The ultimate 'middle child', I was dad's bouncing baby boy number five.

My father John was a teacher of English, no stranger at all to the written or spoken word. He was a loving and attentive father to the most diminutive of his boys. I do believe that when he took in the raucous view from the head of our family kitchen table, he spied the littlest fellow to his immediate left, with a keen and perceptive eye. That table was dominated by the quick wit, sharp minds, and boisterous humor of my older brothers.

Dad seeing this, and my tiny frame, must have thought, . . "this little fella is gonna need some armor." So, he consciously went about on a mission to encourage me to speak my mind, to boldly challenge the older boys for attention at that crowded table, and folks, the rest is history. My history, and hopefully, if you read between the lines, some of your own as well!

Over the years dad and I conversed at great length, on almost everything under the sun. Although it may seem terribly unfair, I was bequeathed perhaps a greater share of his attention, almost, but not entirely by sheer luck. Something about his littlest boy caught his attention and spurred his best paternal instincts. Deserved or not, I was the beneficiary of that attention, and quite frankly, that more than anything else in my life, shaped the man I would eventually become.

My mother Anne, God bless her soul, is in heaven. How could she not be? She raised nine wild urchins as her own mother Molly affectionately used to call us. When dad succumbed to personal flaws, . . . the kind we ALL have somewhere, at some time, she was left to manage the madhouse alone. It nearly killed her as one might expect, but she was an incredibly resilient and strong woman. She passed on to peace and quiet a couple years ago at the age of eighty-eight. I am not sure any person deserved the peace and comfort of heaven more than she, a respite hard earned on this earth. She and I had a most contentious relationship, but one undergirded by very real love, and mutual admiration, despite our often-stubborn refusal to acknowledge it. She once referred to me as 'A giant in a little body', that is how she saw it. I felt that opinion, from the very beginning, and it played no small part in the steady development of my own self-worth and esteem. I learned a great deal from this beleaguered woman, the vast majority of which I was completely unaware of, during the delivering of the 'lessons'!

My eight brothers and sisters, each contributed mightily to my own persona and self-image. Thankfully as a result of an ever-abiding familial love as THE guiding principle from our parents, those contributions were overwhelmingly positive.

My brothers protected me, indulged me, and encouraged me. My younger sisters exalted me, sensitized me, and empowered me. It was sheer luck of a specific birth order that provided me the safest and best place to come of age, at 18 Anchorage Road!

Our little town of Franklin played its part too, and all that came with it. The quintessential suburban bedroom community in Massachusetts in the 1960's and 70's was a place of real wonder, and a community of many good families and friends. America today, could use a little more of old Franklin Mass.

My education began at St. Mary's school, run by the good sisters of St. Joseph. My father's sister Regina was a member of that order. Fortunately for me, she was NOT assigned to my school, but that did not prevent the Vatican pipeline from delivering every report of misbehavior right back to 'crabby auntie sister Regina', and then promptly off to my dear old dad. Nothing at all got by the good sisters!

I truly loved them, even when they had me justifiably by the ear! I remember every single one of them, some admittedly with a bit more affection than others, but all in a light of real gratitude for all they taught me.

The school closed when I had completed 6th grade, and off to the Franklin Public schools I went. I was most fortunate that my 'Irish twin' brother Dave, was right there with me. Eleven months apart, (Richard and Stephen were only ten months apart, have I mentioned my mother yet?) we started first grade together and marched through all of our school years even through college, as a duo. When it was time for Dave to join the older boys at St. Mary's, I realized that I was in a pickle. I asked dad, what am I going to do? I will be stuck at home with all the girls. Dad took me down to meet the nuns, who asked me a few questions, in retrospect, not nearly enough questions, and they decided that I too, was ready for first grade.

I have no doubt that at least a few of them rued that decision for years to come. My older brothers were essentially cherubs who cut a wide path for their mischievous baby brother!

High school and then college at the University of Massachusetts were all that one might imagine they could be in the tumultuous 1970's and early 80's.

Anyway you slice it though, the entire track was one big learning adventure for me.

In my twenties I found myself succumbing to some of the very same human frailties that plagued my father, all neatly packaged in a propensity to medicate my imagined troubles with drink.

The bane of our people, despite all my advantages, I was no exception. That all went to the grave with my beloved father, who passed in 1986.

I was a distraught twenty-six-year-old, but by the grace of God, dad took our mutual afflictions to the grave with him, and my recovery and now thirty-four years of sobriety would begin shortly thereafter.

This however is not a story of struggle, but rather one of joy, so I won't drag the readers through the torment, except to say that it was very real, very difficult, but in the end, just another chapter in a truly marvelous adventure.

In my early thirties I married, we raised three children very successfully and then promptly divorced after twenty-five years. It has been, for the most part, an amicable dissolution. I certainly aim to keep it that way because the work we did do together, does simply astound me. I remain and will forever be grateful to my now 'ex' wife Peggy, for all of the hard work she did, in caring for all of us. That history cannot be rewritten.

Those children, William Alexander, named for my beloved maternal grandfather. Daniel Charles, unmistakably his father's son, and Katherine Rose, the apple of her father's eye, have quite simply been my rai·son d'ê·tre! The English translation or 'reason for living' does not really do the reality justice. Anyone who knows me, understands that completely. I am in awe of them, quite frankly, but their stories are their own to write, and I will leave that to them.

So here we are, in the here and now. In a world gone half mad with Covid-19, political insanity, and social discord of the highest order. What is left for us baby boomers at this point, to hold on to.

I think some careful reflection might be just what the doctor ordered. We, who were born under the promise of the 'New Frontier', had our hearts broken by the turmoil of political and racial divisions of the 60's, survived the malaise and struggles of the 70's, enjoyed the bounty of the 80's and 90's, and have seen the new century get well underway, have a great deal to reflect upon and to be thankful for. We have it seems, lived through the most fascinating of times.

I am called then, by all that I have detailed for you to this point, to somehow try to chronicle our era, our times. The best I can do is to share these following essays, musings, and yes even some poems that I hope others can identify within some portion of their own experience.

My father told me when I was a ten-year old boy, . . . "Every day of your life you will have a choice, you can choose to be miserable, or you can choose to be happy."

"Regardless of the circumstances" he said, "you always have that choice"

I have never forgotten that conversation in our kitchen, early one morning in 1971. Its message became my mantra, and it is my dearest hope that it serves as the same for my own children, because it has served me very well.

I hope readers enjoy this labor of love and gratitude. If you would while reading, try to remember that choosing to be happy IS in fact your own choice, and maybe this work will help provide reason for a few to do so.

Ancestral home in Loughrea, County Galway, Ireland

Where my grandmother was born and lived until the age of 13

Chapter One:

The Irish, those who came before us.

It would require another entire book to tell the whole story of my roots. I have spent many years studying and compiling our family's history that includes nearly a thousand names in the family tree and goes back centuries. That will have to wait for another day. That story is important though, for those that came before us, through their lives, struggles and achievements, most certainly shaped our own.

Ancestral Homelands in the west of Ireland

Our story begins, like that of so many Irish-American families, in the forlorn era and locale of the west of Ireland in the early 19th century. It was there in the storied counties of Cork, Limerick and Galway that our family originates. These were typical poor Irish folk, working the land owned by others and scraping out their lives under the dreary Irish mists. One notable exception occurring in the village of Foynes in the county of Limerick, where the Walsh family did in fact own the land upon which they toiled. The balance of our ancestry however were like the overwhelming majority of Irish Catholics of that time period, tenant farmers who would eventually face the crisis of the potato famine and the difficult choice presented, to wilt and rot like the blackened root, or set out across the seas, westward to the promise of America.

At the conclusion of the American revolution and the start of the new 19th century we find our forebearers toiling away among the peat in villages such as Loughrea and Liss and on the islands in the bay at county Galway. Further north and west, by not too many miles, others forged lives on the busy lanes of Limerick City and on the outskirts in the village of Foynes.

These were the Combers and Hoobans, farmers and fisherman of Loughrea, the Morans of Liss, The Linnanes whose ancient line extends back 1,000 years at Kilcolgan, and the O'Tooles on the islands of Galway bay. The fighting Moores of Scotland resettled now on the lanes in Limerick city, around the corner from St. Michaels parish, and the Genteel Walshes of Foynes on the River Shannon, proud local owners of 33 acres of their own bit o' the sod! Further to the south we find the Harringtons or O Hiongardail or O Hurdail as were the Irish spellings for this ancient clan of the Beara peninsula and Bantry Bay. Alongside the Harringtons who were saddle makers and leather workers by trade in west cork, were the Murphys and Hartnetts. Together all of these proud surnames label our tree's roots that run so deep in the damp soil of the west of Ireland.

I have not yet ventured back to 'the old sod', but that day will come. Some of my siblings have and have shared all that wonder with me. The land of Ireland, so ingrained in the American story, is certainly a central theme in my own. As previously stated, that story alone, would fill another book, perhaps even more verbose, appropriately so, than this one. Perhaps the following tale of just one of my ancestors, my beloved grandmother Molly, will suffice to sketch in just enough of that portion of my heart that lives forever in the green grass and meandering stone walls of the Emerald Isle.

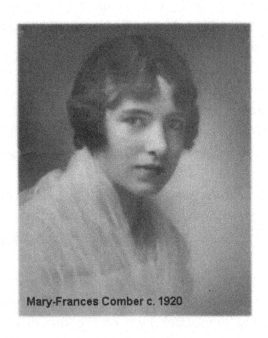
Mary-Frances Comber c. 1920

Mary Frances 'Molly' Comber

She was born at the end of the 19th century, 1898. She used to laugh when I would say to her, Gramma, were you REALLY born in the EIGHTEENTH century???!!!

At 13 years old, she was the eldest of eight children growing up in a small, thatched roof and dirt floored cottage, in the tiny village of Loughrea, just outside of Galway in Ireland. Her father was killed in a 'hunting accident', leaving behind his grieving wife and 8 young children.

As some form of compensation for the tragedy, the wealthy Burke family, for whom her father worked, paid for young Molly to attend 'finishing school' in Dublin for one year in order to learn how to be a 'Lady's companion', . . .simply put, . . . a maid. A trade by which she might contribute to her family's future welfare.

At the tender young age of 14, she set sail, ALL alone, and only shortly after the historic tragedy of the Titanic, for Boston, and America, and a new life with cousins who had emigrated there. It was only shortly after that, that she watched helplessly from across the ocean while her native country, brothers and cousins were all embroiled in the Irish war for independence.
She lived through the first World War, the War to end all wars.
She survived the great Spanish Flu of 1918 in her new home in America.
She fell ill with Tuberculosis in the early 1930's, shortly after her 2nd daughter, my mother, was born. She spent 18 months in 'Quarantine' in a sanitarium on Cape Cod, apart from her husband and two daughters.
She lived through and survived the Great Depression, ever grateful for the opportunities presented in her new country, and mindful of her poor and struggling family back home on the farm in Ireland.
She lived through the Second World War.

She prayed the Rosary every day and each morning, when her husband Bill left the house to fight fires in the city of Boston, she dipped her hand in the holy water dispenser at their home's front door and made the sign of the cross on his forehead. He would then dutifully bow down to receive her kiss on his balding head, before putting on his fedora and heading out to meet the day. She would then return to her kitchen, where only moments earlier, Bill had routinely tossed the saltshaker over his shoulder for good luck while eating breakfast. She would then open the window to toss out any old bread to the 'poor birdies' gathered in the back yard.
She and Bill never owned an automobile, or their own home. They both sent money home to Ireland for all of their lives, and were grateful to be able to do so, and they always managed to keep just a few dollars or coins in their pockets to distribute the their 11 grandchildren and even their grandchildren's friends, whenever they saw them, with a cautionary whisper, "Don't tell your mother I gave this to you"!

Also in her purse she always kept a sleeve of 'Rolaids', . . and she would remind us, ..."These aren't candy dear, they're for me bad 'schtomach' ".

She cried EVERY single time she heard the song 'Danny boy', the heart wrenching ballad of Irish emigration, that became a family anthem.

When her hardworking husband Bill, would come home and retire to his big green recliner in the den, slipping on his glasses to read the latest issue of the 'Irish Echo' newspaper, she would insist that he keep his one beer encased in a small brown bag, just in case company came over. Yet years later, when she was in her late 80's and sitting out in the warm sun watching me, her grandson mow the lawn, . . .she would ask one of my sisters to "Go and get poor Charlie a beer, he's working so hard", . . right out there in broad daylight, . . . company be damned!!!

She knitted countless sets of scarves and mittens, essentially useless against the harsh and wet New England winters, but all worn with great love and pride, by her grandchildren, because of the hands that made them.

In a long life so full of challenge, hardship, struggle and perseverance, she loved poetry, music, romance, God, and her grandchildren, . . . and telling us stories of our Great-Uncle Packy and all of the animals back on the farm in Ireland.

Well into her 80's, after the passing of her beloved Bill, my grandfather, she still walked several miles to attend Mass every morning. She was a lifelong devout and faithful Catholic.

It was on one of those daily treks to church, on an icy winter morning, that she fell and broke her hip. It was time for her to come back to Franklin, the very first place she lived in America, and spend her final years with her daughter Anne and the kids at Anchorage Road. Franklin was the home of her cousin Michael Comber back in 1914, when Molly arrived in America. In a strange twist of fate, nearly fifty years later and nearly just as long after she had left that small town to live in Boston, her daughter Anne and new husband John moved out of Boston to settle in Franklin. In that turn of events, Molly's American adventure had come full circle.

As a girl, she had put her newly acquired skills as a 'Lady's companion' to work for the wealthy Lady Thayer whose family was long ensconced in Franklin Industry.

After a short time, she moved into Boston and eventually met and married her beloved Bill, and they lived in the Brighton section for the remainder of their days together. It was only after her loss of Bill, and the fall on the way to church, that she came once again out to Franklin to spend her last years with us.

It was only a couple more years before God called her home. A life of perseverance, hope, optimism, love, and above all else, faith, had been completed. She left us peacefully in bed at home, surrounded by her daughter, and four granddaughters who took turns holding her hand and telling her how much they loved her as she slipped away.

Tell me again how difficult things are.
Tell me again how unfair our world is.
Tell me again how poor and disadvantaged we all are, ...
And I will tell you nonsense!
Her story is uniquely her own, but there are common elements shared by her entire generation and we would all do well to remember those stories and think twice before ever complaining again.
There have always been heroes among us, . . . Let's promise to never stop looking for them.

I have spent the last ten years working on the Campus of a local independent high school, The Woodstock Academy. Founded at the start of the 19th century, in 1802. This ancient institution has served the educational needs of families in Connecticut's quiet corner for over two hundred years!

Now in the twenty-first century, the school has become the academic home of a substantial population of international boarding students. They come from all over the world to our sleepy little corner, and we and they are incredibly enriched by that circumstance.

In my capacity first as a 'campus safety officer' and then as the steward of the 'Campus store and mail center', I enjoyed daily interaction with these young travelers from afar. A significant number of the students came to us from Asia, China especially. Over the course of the ten years, I made so many special friends and the entire experience proved to be ironically, among the most 'educational' of my life. On the one hand, cultural differences were immediately apparent, and a growing understanding of them was both inevitable, and highly enlightening. Then, conversely, I came to fully appreciate that children, especially, are so very much the same, no matter where they come from or how their own culture shapes them. I honestly grew to love more than just a few of them. Their innocence, genuine affection and most of all courage, made a definite mark on me. These youngsters, aged 14 to 18, were in the final analysis, not very different at all from my own immigrant ancestors who crossed the ocean in search of new opportunities and a better life. My upbringing in a world full of tales of 'the old country', and the consistent melancholy of departure from home, was placed in new perspective by these new young faces who were embarking on a similar and only slightly less dramatic adventure. As a result, my every interaction with them was colored with empathy, and that  is the bridge upon which our beautiful relationships were crossed. I believe that sentiment is well described in this 'farewell letter' to the students that I penned when they all had to go home early in the spring of 2020.

International Students Farewell

To all of you, my friends from all corners of the world,

I am of course saddened by the fact that we will be parting ways so much sooner than expected. I have so very much enjoyed your daily visits to the store and getting to know so many of you, so well.

I wanted to offer a message to all of you, before you leave, about life's challenges and opportunities, and a few things I have learned over my 60 years of living.

Today is St. Patrick's Day, a very big day in my own family, as a result of my Irish heritage. Each year on this day, I take some time to fondly remember those within my family who came before me, who sacrificed and endured so much, so that I, and my own family could enjoy the lives we currently do.

In particular, I often think of my grandmother, her name was Molly, and she was my mother's mother. A little over 100 years ago, young Molly left her home, her mother and 7 younger brothers and sisters and embarked for America. She travelled ALONE, her father had passed away only a year earlier, and as the eldest child, from a very poor family, she set off to make her way here in America, in the hope that she could forge a new and better life, and perhaps send some help back home as well. She was only 14 years old!

My grandmother was a remarkable woman. She was loving and kind, generous and patient, quick witted and fun and was a blessing in the lives of all who knew her. I often imagine how terrified she must have been when she set off for her new country and life here. This was only a year after the historic sinking of the ship, the Titanic, and in fact she sailed for America in boat from the same White Star Shipping company that operated the Titanic. She remained terrified of boats for her entire life, but she came across the wide ocean anyway.

My grandmother faced a multitude of challenges in her life, that lonely trek across a big scary ocean was only the first of many. She survived two world wars, the flu pandemic of 1918, and another epidemic in the early 1930's of tuberculosis, during which she was 'quarantined' for almost two years in a 'sanitarium' on Cape Cod, separated from her family, and her infant daughter, my mother. Throughout all of her long life, she never complained. She saw each and every challenge in life, as an opportunity, and that attitude resulted in a life very well lived, and in the adoration and appreciation of all of us, that followed her.

I share this personal story with all of you because whenever I meet every new group of international students, when I first see your fresh young faces come into my store, I am reminded of my grandmother. I am reminded of her courage, her optimism and her willingness to take on life's challenges and turn them into opportunities. I clearly see so many of you are doing the very same thing, and I admire it more than you probably realize.

I will definitely miss you and am sorry to see you leave early. I will miss your enthusiasm, your good- natured friendliness, your laughter and giggles, and I will even miss your impatience with me, when I cannot find your packages!!!

I will remember you and I will think of you often. I will think of you all also, on St. Patrick's Day, when I remember that brave young lady who left home and family in Ireland. I will remember that you all too possess that same courage, that same willingness to seek out life's opportunities, even amidst it's sometimes frightening challenges.

And I will wonder, . . . I will wonder if perhaps 100 years from now, someone will think of you with great affection and admiration for all that you faced and accomplished, . . .   I am fairly certain they will.

Travel safe and be well, come back and visit when you can, and remember, . . . Be brave, and CHOOSE to be happy!

The genuine friendships developed with these 'temporary emigres' touched my heart, and theirs as well as I learned along the way. I have a wonderful collection of personal notes and little treasure gifts that so many of them gave to me over the years. They were all very serious students, and the road of high school learning, in a foreign language, a thousand miles from home, was to say the least, stressful and daunting for sure. In my little store they found comfort and ease. They came EVERY day, whether they had mail or not. The time spent listening to the old fellow's stories it seems, was a welcome break from a much more intimidating and demanding world. The gift was all mine though, because just as my dad had told me, the extension of love and friendship brings a reward not simply for the recipient, but perhaps even more for the giver. It was indeed my great honor to befriend them and a fitting tribute to all of those brave young souls that came before me as well.

Students Goodbye visit

Plenty of smiles in these photos, but there were also plenty of tears. These are my friends Victoria on my left, closest to the camera, and Kendra on my right with the bandanna on. They came tonight to the store to bring me some gifts, to purchase 'souvenirs' and to say goodbye to Mr. Harrington.

They are both seniors, leaving tomorrow. Kendra was new to us this year, and she explained to me that all of her friends told her she HAD to come to the store, visiting with me was part of their daily routine and they insisted she had to come.
So, she did, whether she had mail or not. Tonight. She told me with tears in her eyes that she knew now, why her friends insisted that she come, she didn't know why at first she said, but now she understands, this literally brought tears to my own eyes.
Victoria, I met four years ago, when she arrived as a freshman. She was in one of my study halls that year. She was only 14, (like my grandmother Molly when she came to this country), she barely spoke any English at all.
She was so quiet and shy, I had to double check to see if she was there during attendance each day. Over these four years we have become great friends. She has been a real joy to me and watching her grow into the accomplished young lady that she is has been an extraordinary privilege.
There are, no doubt, some who scoff at my sentimental musings of this sort. Let them I say, they do not walk in my shoes, but if they did, for just ONE day, they would understand, and they would then wish for ever more, that they did!!!
I truly love these kids, they are infectious!
I will be forever grateful to my friends at The Woodstock Academy, the young ones who fill my heart each year, AND the older ones, who have afforded me this great privilege. I mean it when I say, you really have no idea how fortunate I have been! My time there has brought me full circle, not just to the wonder of my youth, but to the roots of my own family and its emigrant beginnings.

My experience over the years with these young travelers, as well as all the other youngsters at the Academy only served to solidify the lessons my parents had taught me about how best to handle life. The challenges and adversities abound, no matter who we are or where we come from, and they are remarkably universal in nature. It only makes sense then, that our approach to them should be as well. Too often our own biases and prejudices cloud us to the 'universality' of the human condition. Some time spent among children, of all stripes, might very well be the most effective cure, for that affliction.

My Parent's lesson – Joy in the Journey

My parents were both remarkable individuals. Each of them endured significant pain and disappointment in their lives, but neither of them would describe their lives that way, on the contrary they would, if you asked, recount the many great joys and blessings they experienced. Somehow, through osmosis of some sort, but more likely through intent, they passed that attitude on to us, their nine children.

Newlyweds John & Anne Harrington 1954 Cape Cod

It was my father who told me, as many have often heard, to 'Be brave and choose to be happy', that I will always have that choice, regardless of the circumstances. It was my mother who taught me that there is real beauty in ALL of life's living, ALL of it.

She kept a running manuscript for many years, a 'story of her life' that she regularly edited and added to. It was, for many years entitled, 'A journey of Pain', in recognition of all that she had endured. In her final few years, she changed that title to 'A Journey of Love'.

She explained to me that she knew all along that through every moment of difficulty there was great beauty in her life, she would attest to that even in her darkest hours. In the end though she thought it appropriate to re-title her story because the full realization had come to her that every instance of difficulty in her life was the stepping-stone to greater joy and fulfillment. Her final year in fact, may have been her happiest. I am so glad for her, and for me, because the lessons she learned became my own.

Every one of us, if we care to be very honest about it, can look back upon any number of difficult and challenging times in our lives and recognize that these were the days of our greatest personal growth. We often crave the ease and comfort of a fantasy life without turmoil, but if we are honest, we understand that our greatest achievements and satisfaction has come at significant cost to our own ease and comfort.

This is how it works friends, ... When we face adversity, and come through the other side, we can easily overlook all that we have gained in that process. We are often still too close to it, to realize how important that difficult experience will be to us, further on down the line.

It is no wonder at all that a good many older folks seem to stroll around with an air of serenity that mystifies the younger. They have figured it out. Life is NOT a test, (another lesson my Dad taught me), but a gift, and like any gift, it is meant to be enjoyed and used up, . . . ALL of it. The lesson is there for all of us, ... Do NOT despair, work through your challenges and focus as much as you possibly can on the good, the beautiful and the blessings. It will not only strengthen you in those difficult times, but you will fill your personal storage tanks with all the resolve you will need to make yours not a journey of pain, but one of joy!

Chapter Two:

The wide-eyed wonder of youth

The lessons learned while working as an adult at a school brings to mind for me, some of my childhood's fondest memories. Unlike many I suppose, but not all, I simply loved school. I loved the crowd, the noises, the many, many, faces and personalities and of course most of all, ... the girls! I did well enough academically, never really giving my schoolwork the attention it deserved. I was far too busy living the dream. This of course fits right it with what would become my life's 'method of approach'. A zest for experience and an approach filled with 'Wide eyed wonder' was to become my chief "M-O". I sure am glad it did.

Back to School Days

The slight chill and the dewy dampness of the mornings reminds us all that summer is flying on by, . . .I love summer, and mourn to see it go, but now we enter my very favorite time of year. The warm sunny days of September, the cool (mostly) bug-less nights never fail to take me back and wax nostalgic!

It's almost 'back to school' time, and though many dreaded that notion, back in the day, I never did. Living in a small-town population-wise, that covered a fairly large geographical area, meant that seeing friends from school over the summer was often a rarity. In those early years before we all became mobile teens sharing rides in our mother's cars, and before the modern tech of snapchats and tweets, we went those long summer months without the benefit of seeing school chums daily. Let's be honest too, it was mostly the girls I missed!

Many summer evenings were spent imagining what several particularly lovely lasses might be up to at the swimming hole on their side of town, ...come September, and back to school, I was always struck by how much they had grown. Returning to school with their summer tans, in their all new 'back to school' outfits, often with a new, 'grown up girl' hairdos, always gave me pause. I marveled at how they had changed over one brief summer, and it happened EVERY year! . . . and of course, this would be the year 'she' discovered she truly loved me, or at least would acknowledge my existence!!!!

Summertime wanes, and with it those carefree leisurely hours and days. The grindstone of a new school year beckoned, but the blow was always softened by those many lovely faces, hairdos and outfits, completely unaware, or perhaps not, of my admiring eyes. They greeted me, and enthralled me, back at school, every September and I thank them, for the pleasure!

An approach of wide-eyed wonder may be a natural component of youth, I think that is safe to assume. However, that does not mean that it should not be fostered and encouraged. That attitude, if preserved into adulthood can make all the difference in the world decades later. A moment taken to notice and appreciate something beautiful in a day that might otherwise be filled with tedious adult drudgery can be a great source of strength and fortitude to keep us, keeping on. It is important then to note, that preservation of that wide-eyed wonder will not necessarily happen on its own.

It is incumbent upon we the 'adults' to encourage it in our youth in the hopes that they never lose it, and that it will buoy them long, long after we are gone.

The Last – First day of School

It's a bittersweet morning for dear old dad. A watershed moment for sure. I have always loved 'back to school time', even as a little boy. Reuniting with friends, seeing favorite teachers, the excitement of the new year and of course, seeing how much prettier all the girls had become over the long summer were all wonderful ways to start a new year.

New school years took on extra meaning when I became a dad of course, and I reveled in every school year's beginning, with my kids. Every morning during school, for nearly twenty years now I have backed out of my driveway with one, two or three trusty co-pilots in the car with me. This morning I will drive off alone. I will be brave, just like they were. I realize how very fortunate I have been. Thinking back, all the way back to standing in the playground at St Mary's with Billy, clinging to me each morning, and then finally heading off to join his new pals, ... Daniel, seemingly a bit more prepared to run off and join the fray in the school yard, but still looking back at dad for reassurance, . . .all the way to late last spring, when I watched Katherine carrying her clubs as she headed off to play in the Girls state golf championship. A grown woman, heading off to slay dragons, . . .

Each morning trip to school was a mini adventure for me, and one I know not every father gets to enjoy.

So, I will stifle my discontent, and focus instead on my fortune.

I have been so very blessed, starting each of my working days in the very best of company. It really could not have been any better.

Success in school, and in life, starts at home. We have all heard that, but do we know how. What happens at home that makes for success in school? It's not simply about being well behaved, or reading flash cards before pre-school, though those things certainly contribute. In a broader sense not limited to functioning well in school, success in life is greatly determined by self-confidence. That idea too will sound familiar to most. The missing ingredient however, an idea not so often bandied about, would be 'self-awareness'. An accurate and honest appraisal of our own place in the world can give us a much better grasp on how we might make a contribution to it. My children I think possess this self-awareness. Though they are each very humble, and not nearly as boisterous as their old dad, they do seem to have a firm grasp on where they stand, and how they can positively impact the world around them. That quiet almost 'contemplative' nature about them, is not completely unfamiliar to me, . . .well, at least not the contemplative part anyway!

Parenting and Listening

I think it is abundantly clear that I am enormously proud of all three of my children. Why shouldn't I be, they have all done very well. They are bright, hardworking, polite and above all else, kind and compassionate young adults.

I have been asked, more than once over the years, what is the secret? I have actually given this a considerable amount of thought, (no surprise there right?) and this is what I have come up with.

One thing I did learn in my wild college days was the art of 'active listening'. This was a skill set that was part of the required instruction for RA's at UMASS Amherst. Incidentally, the various people and communication skills I was required to learn in that job, proved to be by far, the most valuable things I was taught in college, . . but I digress, . .

Active Listening, . . the formal training I received in college, only reminded and reinforced the methods my own parents used with me growing up, particularly my dad. The bottom line is that whenever I spoke with my parents, I felt as if I had their complete attention. Even in a house with nine wild urchins, I never felt like an afterthought, or a bother, when it came time to speak my mind. My parents, as overwhelmed as they might have been, ALWAYS seemed to make time for me.

In my college years, the formal Resident Assistant training I received stressed that 'listening' well, was not a passive procedure. It required significant focus and discipline. The ability to filter out distractions, our own perceptions and ideas, was a very important part of listening well.

I made this a specific and deliberate part of my relationship with my kids, from the very beginning. The challenge for me was even more significant because of my tendency to carry on, and to literally suck all the oxygen out of any room or conversation. My Irish 'gift of gab' was in this case, a real handicap.

If we ever expect our children to truly learn from our own experience, the first thing we need to accomplish is to get them to listen to our story. That can only be done if FIRST, we have shown them by example, what listening is. Parents, especially younger parents, are often so busy and overwhelmed with all of life's new responsibilities, that we parcel out attention to our children on an 'as needed' basis. Too many conversations happen while we are doing something else.

We might imagine that we are 'multi-tasking' and even pat ourselves on the back for it, but what the children are seeing, AND learning, is how to listen part time, and sometimes to only what it is they want to hear. The relationship between a parent and child is built on the example the parent exhibits, that is how it works from the very beginning, and all the neural pathways are then formed accordingly, . . . IF the parents demonstrate 'active listening' FIRST, the child will follow suit, and then when the time comes for important messages to be transmitted, . . they are more likely to be heard.

Sounds too simple right?

There is something to it, I tell you. How many parents wonder to themselves about their children, especially teenagers, why won't they listen?

When children speak, if they are listened to, . . .FULLY, not while you're doing something else, but given complete attention, they will take themselves seriously and they will learn to do the same with you.

We give a great deal of 'lip service', ironically, to communication these days, but I'm not so sure we aren't kidding ourselves. It's the little conversations through the course of the day, that will make the big difference later on. Put aside the remote, or the vacuum, take a moment to stop whatever else you are doing, and listen, . . the immediate topic might not be of critical importance, but the example and procedure will be, . . eventually.

That's my story anyway, . . and I'm sticking to it!

It all begins of course, in the home. Every childhood, even amongst the most impoverished, Is full of opportunity for wide eyed wonder. If we are lucky, we might vividly remember some of those occasions, and they too will serve us well as bulwarks against a world that too often assails us as adults.

Christmas at Anchorage Road

MaryEllen Harrington c. Christmas 1968
18 Anchorage Rd., Franklin MA

We didn't have a lot of material wealth when I was a boy. Nine children on a schoolteacher salary must have placed a substantial burden on my parents at Christmas time. It's ironic that although I definitely noticed that some of my friends were buried in an avalanche of the latest toys and gizmos on Christmas day, I never really gave it too much thought! Somehow, without knowing precisely how or why, my father's constant message of 'don't measure' (a cardinal rule in a house of nine wild urchins!), had sunk in deeply. I knew every year that my brother David would sneak a peek at his presents, and each year I warned him not to, but he couldn't resist! I knew my grandmother Molly would have some knitted mittens and scarves for all of us, almost completely useless against those frigid snowbound winters of the 60's and 70's, but cherished none the less because we loved her so much that a bag of rocks from her would have been terrific!

I remember one particularly bountiful year, beautiful big fancy three speed blue bikes for David and I. We promptly turned the handlebars upside down so they would look like the fancy ten-speeds of the day! Stephen did get a white ten speed one year, that he METICULOUSLY cared for, for many years afterwards and ultimately led to a life-long passion for bike riding! We had two trees that year, one real and our usual fake silver tree with the gold ball ornaments. Boys gifts in one room under the silver tree, girls in the other, under the real tree. I specifically remember thinking how wonderful it was to have so many siblings that we NEEDED two trees!

I also remember knowing full well, that after the hubbub died down, and my mother's wonderful Christmas dinner was done, that awaiting me in just a few days on the twenty-eighth, was a birthday that my father never once forgot, never once did I get the dreaded 'combo-gift' !!!

I remember clearly that we did not have a lot of money, but far more importantly I remember a house full of love and laughter, my goofy brothers John, Richard, Stephen and David and my lovely sisters, Marybeth, MaryJane, Maryellen and Annemarie, (when 'Annie' came along in 1968, we all implored mom, "Enough of the Marys!", ... she half surrendered anyway!). Dad in his white tee shirt, Mom in an apron, her hair stacked in a bouffant high on her head! Annemarie riding her 'moo-cow', Gi Joes, Barbies for the girls, (and maybe Johnnie too!), ALL kinds of company visiting and each arrival lighting up the house with smiles and good cheer, so very many good family friends!

There were leaner years too, years where I remember being very grateful to the Knights of Columbus as they quickly and discreetly, dropped off a big box full of food, with a HUGE turkey they no doubt set aside for one of the larger families. No we never had a lot of money, but we all knew how blessed we really were, even in the toughest of times every one of us knew we had each other, and that in truth, was the meaning of Christmas, and the greatest fortune of all.

I am grateful to my parents, and to my siblings. I never had a 'bad' Christmas, mine indeed has been a life of great fortune!

Merry Christmas one and all!

Christmas Dinner at Anchorage Rd, in Franklin MA

Those formative years of our childhood, as the descriptor implies, have everything to do with how we will see the world forever more. This is not necessarily however, a 'passive' process. In order to gain access to and take advantage of the strength inherent in the wonders, we MUST remember them, keep them in the forefront of our minds and spirit. It is not a matter of living in the past, but rather a practice of carrying the very best of the past forward and with us every day.

Camp Xavier

My sister Annemarie recently reminded me of Camp Xavier in Center Barnstead New Hampshire. My brothers and I spent the first two weeks of August there every year, I went for eight summers from 7 to 15 years old.

What a wonderful place, some of my very best childhood memories. There were only about 40 or 50 kids in the camp, and the same gang went the same time every year, so we got know each other so well over those years.

Climbing Parker mountain and sleeping overnight at the summit, watching the annual meteor showers under the clear New Hampshire sky. Huge Bonfires on Saturday night complete with the older counselors telling ghost stories about the legendary Perkins family that originally settled the property, the family burial plot was still there, in a mysterious grove of pine trees at the far edge of the camp. When the full moon was just right, the moonlight would shine through the pine grove and illuminate the gravestones, wonderfully eerie!

The camp was run by some extraordinary men, all missionary priests, most from Italy, some brothers and seminarians. They taught me to swim, to canoe, to shoot rifles and pistols. We even made our own shotgun shells. We had outdoor Mass, unheard of in those days, using a large rock as an altar, I took my altar boy classes there. Scavenger hunts, counselor hunts, camper hunts, CAPTURE THE FLAG!, Soccer games, baseball vs the dreaded teams from Huge Camp Don Bosco down the road, hundreds of kids there.

Ice cold soda in glass bottles from the old machine on the main house 'porch', which were later used as 'targets' down at the rifle range, I was deadly with my .22, won more than a few quarters in shooting contests. (10 bullets for .25, I would shoot for money and play all day!), The archery range, a boy Scott from Medway was the best I ever saw, better even than the counselors and priests!

The Mica Mines, Twin Lakes, Blue Job Mountain, Blueberry Hill across the street, what a view that was, (got stung 28 times one afternoon, had to rush to the hospital in the big city of Rochester!) so many pals, The Larsen brothers from Norwood, incredible swimmers, taught me the butterfly, Anthony and a host of others from Medway, the Bradys, Elliots and Rondeaus from Franklin. The Elliots won all the running events in the Olympics, the Larsens won all the swimming. Fr, Benny, Fr. Pete Zannino, Eddie MULE! Brian Casey, Brother Eugene, (Strongest man in the world I thought, and he was in his late 60's at least!), Fr. Lucky Pete Luciano, who swam with a life saver floaty thing around his waist. The Canoes, two birch bark, wide bottoms and one long sleek green one. The Pontoon - we once picked Anthony up in his cot in the middle of the night, carefully carried him out to the pond and set him adrift, still in his cot, on the pontoon!

The Cook's daughter, lil blonde gal in glasses about my age, she was from Medway and as usual, I was smitten! Flag raising in the chilly August air at 6AM, then the mad dash for blueberry pancakes and bug juice! Chicken Barbeques on Sundays, the travel day for weekly campers, old kids out, new kids in. I have never eaten barbeque chicken since, without remembering those Sundays.

I remember my first day, sitting under a tree by the driveway, watching my parents and sisters driving away in the station wagon, I was 7 years old and homesick already and a little frightened of this new adventure. My big brother Rick spotted me, stepped away from the 'big kids' and sat down with me under that big tree.

He didn't say much but must have sensed what I was thinking. "You're gonna love it here Charlie, you'll have a great time", . . .He was so right. I'll never forget Parker Mountain, Camp Xavier and all the great fun I had there!

Those days of youth were not exclusively limited to fun and games. There were of course times for serious contemplation that were no less filled with wonder. Among the most beautiful attributes innate in children, is their capacity AND desire, for learning. In our home, this was indeed a very big deal. My father's Jesuit training at Boston College, and his deep faith and career in education very clearly had an impact on what exactly might fill his children's eager minds with wonder. The mysteries of our family faith were among the primary examples of this. I was completely fascinated by it all, and remain so, even to this day. My own faith is a very private, but precious thing to me. It had its origins I do believe in my own baptism of course, but that was only the very beginning of a lifelong education that on more than one occasion would ensure my survival and success and to carry me forward, all the way to the present day.

Good Friday

When I was a boy, all those decades ago, . . . Good Friday was a VERY important day in our house. My parents were devout Catholics, (which kind of explains the nine kids, well at least partially I guess!) We kids of course loved Christmas, and Thanksgiving for all the toys and treats, but in retrospect, it seems clear that the Easter holiday held an even greater importance to my parents.

They instilled their own sense of reverence in all of us, and never missed the annual opportunity of 'Holy Week' to attempt to provide us with some understanding of the bigger picture of our lives and purpose in this world.

Each year, on Good Friday, we were off from school and promptly at 12 noon, we all retired to our respective bedrooms for a mandatory THREE hours of quiet. The very fact that my mom was able to marshal us all into compliance with this 'tradition', still amazes me! I spent all those Good Friday afternoons on my bed, there was plenty of 'cheating quiet play' for sure, but the fact is, there was also a great deal of thinking, CONTEMPLATION! and even a few prayers.

Somehow, I was able to keep in mind, that those three hours were in commemoration of Christ's time on the cross, with his death coming at 3pm, and the quiet period ending as well.

I suppose in today's world, that kind of parental mandate would be seen as overbearing and even cruel. It was far from it. I know now what a great gift it was. Each year our parents provided us the opportunity to look inward, to properly assess ourselves against the example of living that Our Lord had provided for us.

"There is no greater love, than the willingness to lay down one's life for another" Even as youngsters we could not avoid thinking about what that actually meant. The end result I believe was the learned ability to accept sacrifice not so much as a burden, but as a great opportunity to provide purpose and meaning to our lives. It strikes me as ironic that I lost my dad on Good Friday too. This of course only adds importance to the day and all that it means to me.

If you can grasp at all my thinking, you would understand my conviction that all of it is a neatly wrapped set of messages from the Holy Spirit. Difficult to explain, but it has been the guiding force in my life for all of these years. I am and will forever remain eternally grateful to my parents for these things they taught me. I have not and will not forget them. I wish you all the peace and love of Jesus Christ, and the fullest appreciation and understanding of his 'Good Friday'. May God continue to Bless us all and grant us the good sense to recognize that blessing each and every day.

The rigors of Catholic instruction, and the limitations on youthful exuberance need not stifle the mind or heart of a child. Growing up my world was full of fun and games, and a whole lot of sports. This only makes sense when you count five boys in one house. The competition was fierce and extended to every family in our little neighborhood. We had legends who could hit the baseball clear over the Doubleday's house, (not Abner, mind you, I'm not THAT old!), or barrel through a defensive line in my own backyard all the way through to the street for a touchdown! There were hockey games too, both on the ice on the pond at the bottom of our street, and in the streets themselves when the ice was too thin. Each family in our little neighborhood had at least several children. Our baseball play was so competitive that Scotty and I had to patiently wait on the sidewalk in hopes that one of the older boys might get called home by his mother for some chore or another. That was the only way we were going to get in the game. My brother John, who was rather heavy set in his youth, could hit a baseball a country mile, this despite his propensity to launder the clothes of our many GI Joes, and dance in his room holding a hairbrush to the latest hits from the Supremes. Richard and Stephen too, were great ballplayers, but then it seems at least in my memory, that our neighborhood was full of great ballplayers. Each one a real threat at home plate, looking to drive one deep over what was originally the Conrad's house in left field, later home to ironically, the Doubledays.

In fact, those stories too, of all of the athletic legends of Anchorage road could also fill another book. Our 'extra-curricular' activities however were not at all limited to sports. There were all the usual neighborhood games, hide and seek, capture the flag, red rover, red rover, and many more. There was also music. As an English teacher, dad was involved in a number of theatre productions. We all went to see 'The Sound of Music' on stage, and brothers Rick, Dave and I were even given small roles in Dad's high school production of Macbeth when I was little more than a toddler. My eldest brother John had a wild penchant for music, especially the sound of 'Motown', and Diana Ross and the Supremes. Even I, in all my young masculine glory, must unabashedly admit that due to his persistent influence, I too became a lifelong fan of the lovely Miss Ross.

My dad loved to sing, especially some of the cheesier folk songs of that flowery era, 'leaving on a Jet plane' was a particular favorite, along with the likes of 'Raindrops are falling on my head' and 'Everything is Beautiful'. Mom, although we never saw her play, (not a whole lot of time for it), was a concert pianist as a girl, and even had the honor of playing at Symphony Hall with the Boston Pops as a girl. Stephen, who always carved out his own path, joined the St. Joseph's marching band with his clarinet, and played it pretty well too!

We even had a singing and guitar playing babysitter! A sweet gal of seventeen entrusted with all nine of us wild urchins, her most effective recourse to keeping the boys from literally climbing on the roof was to play her guitar and lead us in singalongs. It worked, at least some of the time. So then amidst all of the rough and tumble of backyard roustabouts, and the strict code of silence on Good Friday afternoons, there was ALWAYS, music.

University of Connecticut High school honors band 2019

I love Music – The importance of the Arts

I love music, always have. I love to sing, even if and when others might not want to hear me! My tastes run the gamut from the folk music I enjoy on my back deck, to of course listening to my daughter play the flute in symphonic band performance of a Russian composer's music, whose name I can not only not remember, but couldn't spell, even if I could!

I was a fan of our own Woodstock Academy music department long before my Katherine started playing with them four years ago, I have attended the annual winter concert for 10 years now, and always thoroughly enjoyed it.

The last few years of course, have been different.

Even in my own advanced years, I understand there are things left for me to learn. I have learned something about school-based music programs that I never fully understood before, and admittedly, took for granted.

In my role as a parent, a father, it was second nature for me to see the many, many advantages that youth participation in athletics offered. I also knew, in an distant, perhaps even aloof manner, that music offered some of those same things to , . . you know, 'the music kids'. What I did not know, until the last few years, was the real extent and depth of it. Over the last four or five years I have seen up close and personally, exactly what kind of impact music education can have, not just on my own daughter, but on a good number of other individual students that I have befriended and gotten to know. It is every bit as remarkable and effective in the development of individual character as any athletic endeavor.

My work at the Academy afforded me an incredible vantage point to witness young people during some of their most critical formative years. I saw them come in as quirky sometimes goofy freshmen and watched them leave four years later having gone through a truly incredible metamorphosis. Perhaps you have to see it from my own perspective to fully appreciate it, but I shake my head when considering it, and the many, many examples I have seen over the years.

I have always known the tremendous impact a good coach can have on young athletes, and in truth, tried very hard to be that coach when I had the opportunity. It is no different for those dedicated musicians who we all see standing in front of disheveled middle schoolers, working tirelessly to try to coax some semblance of mumbling harmony out of the 7th grade boys' choir. Check back on a couple of those youngsters in the back row in a few years, when they boldly perform their solo pieces as High school seniors!!!

More importantly, see, as I have seen, the difference in stride and carriage, the bloom of individual personality and identity and understand this, ...so very much of it comes from the music. The working with others in band or choir, the patient and careful encouragement of teachers, band leaders and choir directors.

Those of you who have watched your own children play or perform, understand this easily I'm sure. A great many of us knuckle-draggers however, though we might well appreciate a 'winter concert' performance, have never fully grasped all that we are witnessing.

So, when the topic of educational costs comes up at your next cocktail party, and questions arise about the cost of 'elective' programs, don't be so quick to weigh in on the cost cutting side, . . . There is so much more to it than 'things for those kids to do' . . . The work is VERY real, the impact is so very much greater than we imagine, and if you are ever fortunate enough to experience it, the results are nothing short of remarkable!!!

__Katherine Plays Danny Boy__

It is difficult for me to explain the profound depth of emotions I experienced at last night's Woodstock Academy Spring concert.

I have been on a hell of a ride of late, my recent health scare of course flashed me back 32 years to the passing of my dear father and yesterday was the exact day, March 28th, a good Friday, that we lost him.

My father's passing marked a watershed point in my own life, and it was not too long after that, that my entire life direction was altered in a way that sometimes I still struggle to fully grasp.

The song 'Danny Boy' has indeed been a 'family anthem' from the time of my very earliest memory. My mother's mother, Molly, loved the song and taught it to each of as babies. It is historically known as 'The' Irish wake song, a tribute to those who left home and family behind to seek a better life in America during the 19th and early 20th centuries.

Molly you see was just one of those millions, the eldest of 8 children, she was sent on her way, alone, the eldest of 8, but only a child of 14, shortly after the passing of her own father whom she loved. She fully embraced her new country but NEVER forgot that little poor village of Loughrea and the family she loved there. She passed that love on to all of her grandchildren.

When she passed away years ago, it was my father who secretly arranged for an Irish tenor to come to the funeral, and unbeknownst to all of us, when the exit procession at the end of Mass began, from up in the balcony at St. Mary's in Franklin Mass, came the richest most beautiful sound I had ever heard, as Molly was serenaded with the song that never failed to make her cry.

The most beautiful sound I had heard that is, until last night, . . .

My children are the lights of my life, unquestionably. They have been a wellspring of joy and inspiration to me from day one. Katherine is my baby, the youngest, and of course daddy's girl. Last night, she played solo on her flute, accompanying a beautiful choral ensemble singing 'Danny Boy'.

The look of quiet and innocent pride on Katherine's face, the warmth of the smile she gave when the director, Ms. Amy Ranta so graciously dedicated the performance to her father, Mr. Harrington, is something I will NEVER forget.

She has always been a marvel to me, as each of them have been. What I have been privileged to witness over these past few years however, in her time at the Academy, simply overwhelms me.

The contributions of so many are too numerous to list, but I am not sure if any could surpass those of Mrs. Lauren Churchill and Miss Amy Ranta and The Woodstock Academy Music Department.

What Katherine has gained through their mentoring, and her participation, simple blows me away. A calm poised and truly humble spirit has been nurtured and developed. Any father with even half a keen eye could not miss it.

I have always reveled in my children's participation in various activities and have not been shy in boasting of their significant accomplishments, these are after all, my life's work. What though, do I know of music???

Not much other than how easily moved I am by it, and what a powerful medium for peace, love and strength, that it can be.

St Mary School, Franklin MA

All of those things from my childhood have contributed mightily to how I see the world today. I would however be highly remiss, if I failed to mention the good sisters of St. Joseph and all that I gained from my experiences at St. Mary's school in Franklin.

Being fully cognizant of their impact, I made a conscious decision to send my own children to St. Mary's school in Putnam Ct, when the time finally did come. I never hesitated about cost, or convenience in that regard. In fact, I took on the role of 'nighttime custodian' in order to help me afford it. I would go into the school three nights a week, after my daytime work in Providence or Hartford, sweep and mop the floors and clean the lavatories. It was, honest to God, a real labor of love. In those quiet hours, apart from my bellowing baritone singing 'Ave Maria' as I mopped the halls, I was able to relive my own St. Mary's experience. It also made me a warmly welcomed member of a beautiful community of families and teachers, all dedicated to the healthy and happy development in faith, of children. Pretty tough NOT to see the wonder in that. My own children absolutely thrived there. They each went on to become not simply good students, but really stellar ones. They devoured learning and excelled in a manner that still fills me with pride.

It was not just academics though. The values they lived there, are now deeply ingrained in their very makeup. They are intelligent, inquisitive, kind, loving, generous, forgiving, and most of all compassionate young adults. So very much of this was honed and developed in that little school. The rest, that perhaps they learned at home, had its origins in another St. Mary's, miles and decades away, in that little town of Franklin. Wouldn't those good sisters who scolded me so often, be pleasantly surprised!

Dear Auntie Sister

Dear Auntie Sister,

   I hope this email finds you well. I was thinking of you this morning and thought I should send a note. This week here in Connecticut we celebrate Catholic Schools Week. At Mass this morning both William and Daniel were specifically selected for participation. They were both Greeters and William read the prayers of the faithful in a clear and steady voice from the lectern.

   A special portion of our celebration was reserved for the Daughters of the Holy Spirit, who celebrate 300 years as a congregation this year. They have been involved with our St. Mary's School for 93 years as well. They were presented with a plaque as well as a proclamation from the Mayor. The Mayor also proclaimed this week as Catholic Schools week in the town in recognition of the fine work being done towards the formation of our community's future leaders.

   Upon arrival in church, little Katherine glanced over at the pew across the aisle where the good sisters were seated and exclaimed to me with bright eyes, "Daddy, look, she looks just like a nun!" referring to an elderly woman in her habit!

   The whole celebration reminded me of course of you and the Sisters of St. Joseph. I said a special prayer in that regard.

   When you do have the opportunity please do convey my thanks and appreciation to your colleagues, most particularly those that taught at our very own St. Mary's of Franklin and most especially to my own Sister Karen who was so very good to me in the first grade, I have not, nor will I ever forget her and our 'Story of Zacchaeus' . Standing on top of her desk in Classroom 1A at St. Mary's, reciting my lines, or 'dancing with her' as she spun me around so high in the air, I thought my feet would hit those circular fluorescent lights that hung from the ceiling!

Assure all of them, that my own children are enrolled and thriving at St. Mary's of Putnam as a result of the profoundly positive experience I had in my own youth at St. Marys' of Franklin. Again, I hope you are well and please do write soon.

with love, your nephew,

Charles

More than anything else, there was laughter. That is what I remember most vividly from my youth. The unending, rip-roaring, almost crippling, laughter. Despite all of the challenges we faced, that noisy cacophony of giggles was, it seemed, ever present.

Those who knew my family in those days will attest to it with solid conviction, . . . we were a funny lot! We had stacks of Bill Cosby albums, which I still have some of today, a favorite too was Vaugh Meader's LP comedically portraying the Kennedy White House, featuring skits like. . ."It's the Hungarian Ambassador for Dinner", . . . and "The Rubber duckie, is mine". We easily could have put together our own Comedy album just from the material generated at our evening dinner table. My parents both had a terrific wit, and my older brothers had us in stitches all the time. It was Dinnertime jokes neatly wrapped in stories of the day's events, that were most urgently encouraged. As the youngest boy, I was always over-eager to participate, and tossed out more than my share of 'droll bombs', but led by my father in a roar of "Flags go down", the family responded enthusiastically anyway, and I was none the wiser, only thrilled with the roar of the crowd. Laughter, especially in the face of turmoil, really is the best music of all, and our home then, and my own home now, I am very pleased to say, have not seen any shortage of it, at all.

Those carefree and yes wide-eyed times of youth are the fuel that feeds us all. We all then should take whatever time is necessary to make sure we keep the tank of memories full, and by all means continue to generate more for the days ahead.

Perhaps nothing in my memories of laughter stands out more, than those many times we sat around the table listening fervently to my eldest brother John regale us with some tale or another. He and my sister Maryjane, she of the fiery red hair, were our very best storytellers. In those roles they also by far, generated the most laughter. This only makes the vacuum created by their early passing that much more obvious to those of us that remain. My grandmother would call them "real pips", but I can still hear their voices, and the roomful of laughter that so often accompanied them.

Johnnie's Laugh

Johnny, Johnny . . . don't we all know

how johnny loved to laugh . . .

Of all the things he did so well,

and many that they were,

The thing our johnny did the best

Was when our johnny laughed.

Return us now to Anchorage road

around the kitchen table,

A cigarette, . . .a story told,

His mouth agape,

the tears they rolled.

We little ones will say once more,

Tell us Johnny,

tell us more.

But Johnnies died,

and we've all cried,

Where's the joy in that?

The joy in that,

is in the fact,

we all heard johnny laugh.

So wipe your tears and grieve no more,

remember to laugh,

laugh like before.

Smile for him, and laugh for him

and our Johnny will laugh

forever more.

Chapter Three:
Coming of Age

The decades following our formal education do not and should not mean the end of learning. Quite the contrary in fact. Especially those years when we really do start to strike out on our own. Our twenties are more often than not, the most tumultuous years of our lives, they certainly were for me!

l to r; Brother Dave, Bill Brunelli, himself, Scotty LaRosa and Mark Healy c. 1980, Best of pals for over 50 years

The preparations had all been made, the groundwork laid firmly and as my dear mother would say, "the seeds have all been planted".

In Your Twenties

As my children now are entering their twenties, with the end of formal schooling perhaps approaching I am compelled to remind them of what I learned AFTER school. Looking back at my own twenties now, with the benefit of 30 plus years of hindsight, I realize that the REAL learning began and was most intense during my twenties.

Striking out on your own as a young adult, hopefully armed with tools provided through years of formal schooling, our twenties are the time we learn how to make proper use of those tools.

I realize now, that the period from my mid-twenties to early thirties were perhaps the years I actually 'learned' the most. This was certainly not intentional on my part, and too much of the learning might have been done 'the hard way', but none the less, in retrospect, it was a most productive period.

In your twenties, the priorities become your own, not your parents or school system's.

Choose wisely how you spend your time and expend your energy. There is and should be fun to be had for sure, . . . but in the midst of it all it would be helpful to remember that these are the years that YOU will shape your future from. Up until this time, the future has likely been shaped for you, but now YOU get to decide how and when to alter course. When you get old and gray like dear old dad, you may very well look back on this period and realize that it was at THIS time, YOU decided, who and what you were going to be.

I am envious, . . .it is a wonderful opportunity, made even sweeter perhaps if you are fully aware of the possibilities.

By all means enjoy this time to the fullest, ... BUT LEARN, LEARN, LEARN, . . . everything you can, about EVERYTHING you can.

The knowledge gained during this pivotal period of your life will serve you so very well, for all of the rest of your days, . . . I guarantee it!!!

Things I miss, . . .

We lead such busy lives in this day and age, I remember a much slower time.

I miss Sunday morning newspapers that were so voluminous that they came in three sections and took almost all day to read. On Sunday mornings the day's neighborhood deliveries would completely fill the back of the family Country Squire wagon and we boys would pile in as well in order to get them all delivered in time to go downtown to Sunday Mass.

I miss Friday nights with the boys, getting all worked up for adventure, deciding where to go and what to do, fully convinced that all the lovely young ladies were out there waiting for us all!

I miss stopping at 'Down on the farm' for a beer after work and some pleasantries with Joe or Emma Halligan, "All in the family" on the television behind the bar, . . truth be told I too often stayed right through dinnertime, but none the less, . .

I miss scrambling to get ready for work in the morning, because I was out too late, and Brian Woodman waiting always patiently in the driveway at 7:10 sharp, and always with a coffee in hand, . . .

I miss the excitement of a future ahead of me, the vim and vigor of my early twenties, opportunities abound and too many choices to make.

I miss Old Cape Cod, when it was much quieter, only 50 minutes to the beach in Dennisport, where again all the lovely young ladies were waiting just for myself and my pals. One gal in particular, all the way from Needham Mass., but summering each year in Harwichport, held my hearts attention for three successive summers where good fortune had shined on me and we spent plenty of time together in the salty air.

I miss all those heavy philosophical discussions, often under the stars, as we tried to 'figure it all out', fully convinced that we were doing so too!

I miss the excitement that came with the prospects of a paycheck with 40 hours of overtime, . . .double shifts were definitely worth it, though for the life of me I have no idea where all that money went!

I miss Harry and Elsie, whose beautiful daughter captured my heart in the early 80's. They were beyond welcoming and kind to me, even when their daughter was away at school, I still spent a great deal of time at their home in Framingham. I often played cards with Elsie, and learned to play golf with Harry on the 14 hole Millwood farms course just a mile or two from their house. I'm not sure any 'boyfriend' ever had it so good with his girl's family.

I miss my long red hair, . . . the same hair Harry was quick to notice when I first met him. I worked with both Elsie and her daughter, my sweetheart Janelle, and as such I was perhaps a bit too comfortable when I first went to the house to meet Harry. He had been out mowing the lawn. When he came in perspiring and tired, he sat down across from me in the living room and the first thing he did was pose the question; "So tell me young fella, about how much do you spend a year on haircuts?" Looking back at him and taking note of his balding head, I confidently and wryly replied, "I'm not sure, but I am guessing it's probably about the same that you spend on shampoo". I honestly didn't know if he would throw me out then and there, or if the gals would have to rush to my defense. He grinned back at me however, and asked, "Do you want a beer?" That little parlay led to a solid friendship that lasted even well beyond my dating Janelle. These were extraordinary people, and extraordinary times.

Don't misunderstand, I'm a happy fellow and am ever grateful for the many blessings I have been given. But if I told you I didn't miss my youth, . . .I'd be lying.

Although my father had left the family home when I was in junior high, moving to a small apartment about five miles away in downtown Franklin, he remained very close in our lives, and certainly so in mine. His passing of sudden heart failure was, I believe, a line of demarcation for us all. His death, quite literally shattered me. Up until that point, I was functioning fairly well for a 25 year old, my energy and exuberance sufficiently covering for my own human frailties that would soon overcome me. It was only a few months after his passing, without his presence over my shoulder, that I had tailspun into what many of those closest to me saw as a slow, but inevitable death spiral. That was not to be however, by the Grace of God, I was lifted out of that dark destiny, and quite literally saved in the nick of time.

This following poem came to me in a dream, a few years after his passing. I was living alone, in a bachelor studio on Cape Cod. I woke up at 3 O'clock in the morning, sat down at a typewriter and banged out these words, exactly as they appear now.

Sons of Dad

Aptly named might we be
Sons of dad
Brothers and me.

Baptist John who paved the way
Dad we mourn, he called friend.
First born, first torn,
A hope a heart,
Someday to mend.

A source of strength when all's apart,
Richard Michael, Lion heart.
Unto his banner others drew,
Into their hearts, his courage flew.

Stephen Edward, regal heir,
The road he walked, no others dared.
Alone he struggled, alone he fought,
A home a castle, his hands have wrought.

David William, beloved one,
A prince, a lamb, a heart undone.
A quest for love that knows no end,
A hope, a heart, someday a friend.

Charles the Great, no Roman King,
Of sons and clan his heart will sing,
Caesar not his destiny,
but proud of all he will be.

Aptly named might we be,
Sons of dad, Brothers and me.

Each day, bit and tad,
Each year, more like dad.
Look around that you may see,
Aptly named,
Sons of dad,
Brothers and me.

That poem marks the time I believe when my real understanding of the bigger picture in life truly began.
The gravity of all that I had been through in the decade of my twenties was crystalizing in my mind. This began in me, a growing awareness and appreciation for what I was coming to understand as a miracle.

A further effect was a maturing perspective on those closest around me, a surprising and gratifying number of whom had held on to me, through the entire ordeal. These were my closest friends, a wildly diverse group of guys and gals, who despite my many shortcomings, never really did give up on me. A few more years on, we all got in the habit of getting together annually, for a raucous dinner date filled with stories and laughter, reliving of our glory days, and maintaining the bonds that held us close. It was at one of those dinners that I delivered to them, this following message, straight from my heart to all of theirs.

25 years and more

Twenty-five years ago, in 1976, we were all friends. Some of those friendships were in their infancy, and who knew then how well they would endure. There were already, at that point in '76, friendships that were a lifetime long. Scott, and I, Mark and Eddie, Mac and Johnny, Bill and John and of course, Robin and Susan. Some of these pairings now approach 40 years each!

In my own case, I truly do consider myself blessed to have enjoyed these remarkable friendships over such a long period of time.

I played with Scott as I learned to walk, I played 'Red-Rover, Red Rover' with Mark and Bill as I learned to read, and played the teenage fool with Mac, John and Johnny, as I learned to work.

We were all together when John and Trish got married, the first of all of us!

We have climbed mountains together, literally, at Tuckerman's ravine. We have sung together at so many concerts and swam and sunned together on so many beaches.

We certainly have drunk, and been drunk together, some of us even got sober together!

We have lived, laughed and done our share of crying together over these 25 years and more.

We have had children, and we've watched them grow together. It is not a stretch to assume we will see grandchildren together.

We are indeed a lucky and special bunch. Outside of this group, how many people do you know who have been this fortunate. Maintaining life-long bonds such as ours, with such a diverse and large group of friends takes special effort, by special people.

Though we may find the endeavor effortless at times, each of us at some point has been called upon to be patient with another, to forgive another, and yes to endure another, for the sake of the whole. I know I certainly have tested these bonds, perhaps more than most and maybe that is why it falls to me to remind us all of our good fortune.

Ultimately for twenty-five years and more, we have cared for each other, for that we owe each other, and God, our thanks.

The Irish have a long and splendid tradition of oral history. This of course is an important part of my heritage and as such I am compelled, as I have always been, to remember and record. It was perhaps Scott's mother Lillian who first offered the assessment, "He has the gift of gab". And that was probably over 35 years ago!

I offer then to you my friends, in the fashion of the Irish whose oral history dealt so often themes of friendship and family, of loyalty and honor, . . .a poem.

Though I wrote this particular poem about one specific pair of lifelong friends, the gist of it certainly applies to all of us.

Consider this, when I do write poems, they are written directly from my heart. In writing and in reading and sharing this with you, I hope to remind you all that I love you and cherish our friendship, and remain eternally grateful for all of its blessings.

Little Old Men

Two little boys, red and blond.

Through all the years, a lifelong bond.

Quick and bright, frail and wild.

Sure and calm, firm and mild.

Tricycles, bicycles, adventures galore.

Tonka trucks and baseball cards

And so much more . .

Two young men together again

Through all the years, the best of friends.

Girls and games, on the run.

Fast and fun, almost undone.

Two grown men, through thick and thin.

Tee to green and around the bend.

Little ones of their own and families to tend.

Fathers and friends, all over again.

Little old men who shuffle along.

No longer those boys , red and blonde.

As close as brothers, though worlds apart.

A lifelong bond, forged in the heart.

I think it is fair to say, that our close knit gang of thieves were loosely built on a pyramid of three pillars. Those three, whose initial connection began in very early childhood, were the tripod upon which all the strings of friendship were interwoven. Scott, in the poem above, myself of course, and our sturdy third leg Mark were essentially at the center of all of the orbits of this wonderful community of friends. Where Scott had been my trusted lifelong companion, ever kind, ever calm, my Samwise Gamgee of sorts, Mark was the solid rock upon which I rested when weary. Like Peter the Apostle, the rock upon which the church was built, it was in some ways upon this rock that my own faith in myself was rebuilt. In my darkest hours Mark never faltered and never gave up on me. These two heroes would both need those same qualities of character later in life, facing very significant challenges of their own and though I was never quite surprised at their strength, I was indeed comforted and inspired by it, and still am. I think I explained it well in a birthday note to Mark just a few months after the passing of his forever love and wife of 37 years Susan.

A Birthday Greeting for a lifelong Friend

We have been best pals for over 50 years. We met at Scotty's when I was about 4 years old, then ended up in first grade together at St. Mary's in Franklin. We tormented our friend Bill in the playground there, hoping he would never catch us, we were quick and wily, and he was the only kid I knew who could keep up with my hyper-energy.

At Franklin High school I convinced him to join me on the wrestling team, sharing the lightest weight class with me, he was the toughest damn competitor I ever faced, much stronger than I, and never willing to give up, he made me work so much harder than I would have without him and his tenacious competition helped make me a very good wrestler.

We chased girls together, and double dated with two lovely gals to our Junior prom, and even had a police escort because we were late and got lost on our way there! Then off to Horseneck Beach to watch the sun rise, ...

We spent our early twenties building houses together and keeping up with him working, was nearly impossible. We vacationed together every summer on Cape Cod, with his lovely sweetheart, then bride Susan, who I simply adored. When they married, I took the liberty of 'moving in' with them for a month or so, just to help them get started, ... (Ha!)

A few years later, when I was at my lowest point, he was perhaps my 'friend of last resort', never abandoning me, always checking in with me. I will never forget his concern and kindness and am still very grateful to this day.

In over 50 years, we have never had cross words, not even once, ... and I'm sure I provided plenty of opportunity, ...

This is my lifelong friend Mark Healy, one of the very finest men I have ever known. I truly love him like a brother, and I know a thing or two about brothers, ...so if you see this handsome fellow today, wish him a very Happy Birthday, and if he is a friend of yours too, take a moment to remember how very lucky you are, I know I will!

If you're feeling brave, go ahead and challenge him to a game of 'hand slaps', he can't beat me, ... but I guarantee neither you nor anyone else will EVER beat him, even if you take the skin right off his hands, ...

Happy Birthday old chum. I know it won't be your best one, but you are loved and admired and always in my heart and prayers, and I remain forever grateful for your true and enduring friendship, rock solid, over all these years.

These friends, such a wide variety of personalities and demeanors, and my growing sense of appreciation for them, would be instrumental in my future interactions within my own family. In each of my children I could of course recognize snippets of both myself and their mom, but ultimately, what I saw best, and came to appreciate most, was those parts of them that were entirely unique to themselves. I gained this vision through these friends, and from their unique contributions to my coming of age. It has allowed me to see things in my own children, as they have matured, that I otherwise might not have known. Additionally, it is through the lifelong lens of these friendships, that I have perhaps most clearly been able to 'cherish every moment'. A point brought home to me just a year ago, during the stage production of the Thornton Wilder play, Our Town in which I was privileged to be cast in the lead role. Cherishing every moment of life is the principle message from Wilder. This is perhaps best exemplified in young Emily's crucial line, "Oh, earth, you're too wonderful for anybody to realize you. Do any human beings ever realize life while they live it -- every, every minute?"

What goes around, comes around, . .

The cast of 'Our Town' from The Woodstock Academy Production

One of the unforeseen treats of the whole 'Our Town' experience for me has been performing in front of my children while they sit in the audience.

On each of the last two nights, the boys, Billy and Daniel, have been in the audience with their respective sweethearts, both gals I like very much, and noticing them out there slightly jarred me from my hard fought concentration on the 'role'.

Mind you, I'm not complaining at all. On the contrary, I am quite tickled by the whole thing.

Turnaround is fair play isn't it? In a way this is payback for all those times when one of them was in a position of the limelight, and there was dear old dad, prominently and unabashedly basking in their glow, and undoubtedly adding a bit of pressure to the whole situation. Such has been the case for their entire lives and boy didn't I thoroughly enjoy it! Now the tables have turned a bit, tonight my Katherine will be out there in the seats for this final performance, and the prospect fills my heart to the brim.

It's a great play, a terrific role, and I am proud and grateful for this wonderful opportunity.

My children certainly know well enough to fully appreciate the profound message of this play, they have, essentially, been lectured on the same message for their entire lives.

They are also smart enough, and intuitive enough to realize how and why it all means so much to dear old dad.

They get it, . . . they are wonderful, . . . and I am blessed and love each of them all the way to the moon and back again! ,. . . For every, every minute!

Chapter Four:

Sobriety

Three chapters in, and the reader must wonder was it ALL unicorns and rainbows? certainly not. The decade of my twenties, the 1980's was one filled with personal turmoil and ultimately, personal growth. The changes wrought during those times, were perhaps the most profound of my sixty years. The passing of my father marked the start of a period that appeared initially hopeless, then ultimately involved miraculous maturation. It was a period that started in crowded bar rooms and ended in the quiet solitude of a studio apartment on Cape Cod. Those environs in many ways, accurately depict the state of my soul at that time. Once again it occurs to me that the subject matter of this particular period, on its own, could fill yet another book. That too will have to wait. Suffice to say that it was in 1986, in the middle of my twenties, that both my father and my drinking, died. Those two events spurred within me the greatest of all the changes in my life, ultimately much for the better. I begrudgingly gave up the alcohol at first almost to spite my poor mother, but in the end to sanctify her. I will state for the record here, in print for all the world to see, . . . She was right, and I was wrong.

Twenty-eight years

Twenty-eight years in the life of a 54 year old is a long time, just over half of my days. It' an important milestone for me, one I hope to share without being 'preachy'. November 6th, twenty-eight years ago, was the last time I had an alcoholic beverage! That day of course marked the most significant change I have ever made. I was 26 years old, and things were not exactly going well.

I had no one to blame but myself, bad choices, a bit of hard luck, some naiveté, and a natural youthful supposition of invulnerability all contributed to my dilemma. To be clear, I suffered from no disease, my parents didn't ruin me, the world was not unfair to me, my friends did not abandon me, quite the contrary in fact, up to that point I had actually been blessed and very fortunate. I know that now, though I had trouble seeing it then.

I loved to party and still do!, who doesn't? The problem was that I had fallen into a trap where I became convinced that the only way to party, to enjoy, was to be in an altered state. The question of why finally occurred to me. What was wrong with just plain ol' me, that I needed to supplement the original me with the enhancing effect of alcohol or drugs. It occurred to me that I was slowly but surely losing that 'original' me. That became unacceptable because quite frankly, despite all of my shortcomings, I liked that guy, AND, so did a lot of other people! He was quickly fading though, being replaced by someone sad, angry, and not very fun to be around. He was saved, with the help of a strong faith, and the support of some very good people. I was very lucky and have seen far too many who were not.

I do not believe life is a test, rather it is a gift, meant to be enjoyed. The gift however requires care. My Dad said that you don't leave a new bike out in the rain to rust, you have to take care of it to fully enjoy it. It took me over a quarter of a century to figure out what that meant. Our lives are our own, what we make of it entirely up to us, no one else. We have choices, and there are consequences to them. None of us is 'locked in' to any given course. When someone tells you nothing can be done, it can't be helped, or you have no choice, NEVER believe them! My father instructed me to 'Choose to be happy', I finally did, twenty-eight years ago on November 6th, 1986. I have been, for the most part, ever since. Those who know me best, know the entire story, they know the truth of it.

I will be forever grateful for the love and support of all of them. The very fact that so many stood by me is a testament to the fact that mine was a life worth saving, worth living, and every victory, every accomplishment and every joy, I share, with them.

This 'miracle' of course, was not my doing. Though I was certainly not fully aware at the time, the hindsight of 20/20 vision and a clarity of mind eventually enabled me to see and remember so many people who played a part in my 'salvation'. There were so many, and I do remember them and remain eternally grateful to them. Ultimately though, like so many of the other watershed moments of my life I have to give final credit to what I have come to understand as the almighty grace of God. That is not simply a cop out, or the wild assertion of a born-again bible thumper. The transformation and process involved, that I do believe remains ongoing, was so complex, so grandiose, that I really cannot think of it in any other way. Perhaps you would have had to live it yourself to fully understand that, I did, and that is exactly what I believe.

Stick with The Winners

Over thirty years ago, a very wise, serene, and compassionate older gentleman I knew gave me a very valuable piece of advice.
He told me, "Charlie, stick with the winners".

We, and our lives, are a reflection of the choices we make, and one of those choices is when we decide who we associate with, who we include in our 'inner circle'.

Who are the winners? The winners are the folks who wear the face of serenity, wisdom and compassion that this man did. They are the folks who walk through life concerned first and foremost with their own business, their own goals and aspirations, their own work and family, their own strengths and weaknesses.

The winners are too busy forging their own success and peace of mind to meddle in the affairs of others. They are too busy with self-examination and betterment to focus on criticizing others.

They are humbled too much by their own shortcomings and human frailties to spend any time pointing out the faults of those whose lives they are not living.

Winners avoid the gossip, whispering, and scheming that so many revel in, they simply do not have the time or inclination. Managing their own lives both fully occupies them and satisfies them.

The winners, sleep well at night, contented by the honest knowledge that they are doing the best they can with life's everyday challenges.

They are the friends who rather than advise us on what THEY think we should do, remind us by their example, of what we all know is right and wrong, and what we actually should do. They have no need of secrecy or trickery, no need to win or 'put one over' on anyone because they live by a code that concerns their own behavior first.

When I would complain to this gentleman about all the people in my world who made things tough for me. . as I often did in those days, ... he would gently suggest I stop looking at them and start looking at me.

It was honest, direct, and very helpful advice, and I remain grateful to him for it. He's been gone a long time now, but I haven't forgotten his words, and more importantly, his example.

Rest in Peace Kenny Moore, you were a great friend to me, . . .and still are.

To illustrate the ongoing presence of that Grace of God in my life, I need only to remember when I suffered from my own heart problems, remarkably similar, and at the precise same age that had taken my father from me. Coincidence? Perhaps, but I will leave that for the readers to determine for themselves.

It was just not my time

Is every day precious? .... you bet your sweet you know what it is!

We cannot live in fear, the world and all of our lives are filled everyday with enormous risk, no more now than it has ever been. Each year, roughly 50 million people die in this world, when our time has come,. . our time has come.

At the same time all of our lives are filled with tremendous opportunity every day, more so now perhaps than at any time in the long history of mankind. Each year roughly 150 million babies are born. Life is still winning, . . .by a three to one margin.

At six years old I had a very bad allergic reaction to a bee sting. Stepped on a bumblebee in the backyard and later that night when changing into my pajamas for bed, my brother Dave noticed enormous hives all over my body. I was taken to the hospital around midnight, the doctors told my mother that if I had gone to sleep, I likely would never have woken. It was, however, not my time.

A few years later I was stung again, 28 times running through a bee's nest on a blueberry picking adventure at a remote summer camp in New Hampshire. The camp maintenance man raced me to the hospital in Rochester, a good 40-minute drive in his AMX Javelin hotrod. When we reached the emergency room I was choking for air, . . . but it was not my time.

At twenty years old I was in a horrible car accident. Fell asleep at the wheel and drove off the highway in New Hampshire at 3 AM, (maybe I should just avoid New Hampshire???), the car was a 1974 Ford Pinto, the blowup model. It ended up lodged in a tree and had to be secured there with ropes before they extricated me from my seat. I had a broken arm, and a badly broken nose from hitting the steering wheel. I was unconscious for three days, and my mother had our family priest come and deliver the last rites over me in my hospital bed, . . .but it was not my time.

My twenties were filled with close calls and my best friends all had imagined I would never see 30, but they were mistaken because it was not my time.

Almost a decade later at 28 years old I was working in Europe, travelling frequently on airlines. On the way home for Christmas, from that first trip to Europe, I was bumped from my seat at Heathrow Airport in London because the flight was overbooked. I was delayed about an hour, and flew home, first class on British Airways instead. . . . .My original flight was to have been on Pan Am, . . . flight #103, . . .That flight went down over Lockerbie Scotland and all 270 people on board died, . . .but it was not my time.

In my thirties, I was travelling on route 20 in Auburn, returning home from a day trip and headed to 4 O'clock mass at my parish in Southbridge when a young man ran a red light and smashed broadside into the little Dodge Neon I was driving, completely totaling the vehicle. It scared the living daylights out of me, but I walked away without a scratch. . because it was just not my time.

In my early forties I was driving home from a monthly board meeting in upstate New York. It was winter and there had been a messy mix of rain and snow for the entire trip home. Upon crossing the border from Mass into CT on Route 169 in Southbridge, my Nissan Pathfinder hit a snowbank in the middle of the road that had been deposited when the plow had reached the state line and turned around. I lost control and the vehicle did at least one complete 360 before falling off an embankment and then rolling over and over down to the bottom of a ditch. When I finally stopped rolling, every window was smashed but the engine was still running. I said a frightened and sincere prayer of thanksgiving and then proceeded to use the four wheel drive to climb out of the ditch and limp home, . because it was just not my time.

A few years ago, I sat on the edge of my bed on a Friday evening not feeling well at all. A strange but not brutal discomfort in my chest, combined with a strange numbness in both of my elbows and some shortness of breath had me very concerned. I was 56 years old, same as my dad when he had suffered a massive heart attack that took his life. Cognizant of that fact, I decided to drive myself down the road to the hospital. I had a coronary artery with a severe blockage and just like that first incident with the bee sting 50 years ago, if I had gone to sleep, I likely would never have awoken.

It was just not my time.

So, when folks think I'm being corny or overly preachy when I go on and on about choosing to be happy or living each day as a gift from God, I suppose that is ok. They have not travelled my road.

I have however and that road has convinced me that every day is indeed a gift and I will be damned if I am going to live it in fear, just in the hope of making it to tomorrow.

We all have our own appointment with the end, but very few really know when.

I intend to keep that in mind and when I feel like complaining or become dissatisfied with my station in life, when I think for a moment, as we all have done from time to time that life is terribly unfair, I will try to remember all of those 'times', that were simply not 'my time'. Then I will thank God for another day, another gift, and for all those previous days that I have been given.

It really is all about perspective folks, ... Carry on and live courageously, because today is very likely,

Just not your time.

Given so many chances to get things right, to live in a manner that honored all that I had been given, it became apparent that returning to the values of my youth was the only way to do so. A clear head, and a grateful and contemplative mind can lead only back to the very basics that formed us. We all get lost in the clutter of day to day living and doing so presents us with innumerable opportunity to stray from the path we know to be the right one.

Our modern world too, is a place of overwhelming distraction and temptation, and I think it likely this is not accidental. There is sadly, a lot more profit in the sins of mankind, than in his virtues.

Do the Right Thing

We live in a world of self-inflicted drama and misery.

At a time where virtually everyone we know should be humbly thanking God for the many blessings and good fortunes they take for granted, people are so self-involved, so caught up in their own selfish concerns, they are miserable.

This age of 'moral relativism', where everything is 'ok' as long as it makes us 'happy' is all one big lie.

In fact, it works precisely to convince us we are NOT happy and builds within us a resentment against the world for making us so. There is right and wrong, good and evil, despite our desperate attempts to ignore those age-old truths.

Now many will balk at this suggestion, but the biblical messages of 4 thousand years have told us that our worldly pursuits are the playthings of the devil, and that this world we live in is his domain. When our life's focus is on this world and its 'manufactured' pleasures, the result is turmoil and dissatisfaction that can never quite be sated.

The rules for living a successful and happy existence are the same as they have always been, and they are based on moral and ethical principles that sadly we have concluded are 'out of fashion' and no longer meaningful. After all, you can't find them on Amazon so really, of what use are they?

The answer for a 'good night's sleep' and a hopeful start to each new day, is quite simply, to do the right thing. It is in fact so simple and straightforward that it is just mind boggling that so many cannot grasp it.

It is true that 'doing the right thing' is not always the easy thing, that too is an age-old truth. The fact is, however, that with consistent practice and effort, it gets easier over time. Ours though, is a terribly selfish and impatient world, we want everything we want, and we want it right now dammit!

And so, we convince ourselves that cutting corners, taking the easy road, ignoring the moral and ethical questions that might give us pause, is the way to go, . . . and we end up chasing the fantasy that if we can continue to fool ourselves we will reach nirvana.

It is all a fool's errand, but in our modern age, we are too stubbornly devoted to 'our' needs, to admit that. We have been taught over lifetimes, that nothing we have is good enough. This of course is directly contrary to the reality of our lives, especially in this country and time.

We enjoy a standard of living and creature comforts our grandparents could hardly imagine. The television ads though, tell us we don't have enough. We can't possibly be happy or fulfilled unless we go out and buy the latest whatever.

Our self-worth and the value of our existence is determined by the number of likes and the comparisons we see on social media, and never by honest Self-examination of our own real life and circumstances.

We complain that we are not happy, . . . and we blame the entire world. The truth is that we have no one to blame but ourselves. We are chasing the wrong ideal. 'Happiness' is fleeting, life can sometimes be difficult, for everyone and anyone. What we should be seeking is peace of mind, peace of the soul, a peaceful night's sleep and a peaceful start to each new day. You won't see any television commercials or articles in Glamour magazine promoting that idea, but it is the secret to living well and no amount of partying or spending of money will ever replace it.

There is only one path to finding that inner peace, to living that life of 'real' satisfaction, and that is the path of righteousness, nothing else will get the job done. To be kind, to be honest, to seek forgiveness when we have wronged, to be responsible, to honor our obligations and be trustworthy, to help those in need, without expectation of reward, to concern ourselves with the 'business of mankind' as old Jacob Marley said to Ebenezer, in the classic 'Christmas Carol". These are the points on our personal checklist that matter.

As long as we seek first to make ourselves 'happy', we will come up short and disappointed because if I have learned one thing in my almost 60 years, it is that happiness is fleeting, but peace is eternal. The former can only be appreciated, if the focus is on the latter.

So maybe it has almost all been unicorns and rainbows after all! At the very least one can say that I have been granted a sufficient dose of the 'Luck of the Irish'. I don't quite see it that simply though. My own conviction is that I am here for purpose, and that purpose no matter how inadequately I might attempt it, is not of my own design. Just as my entire life has been so strongly influenced by the teachings from the best part of my father, so too has it been influenced by all of his human frailty. Long ago, without fully intending to, I set on a course of atonement for those frailties I so clearly recognize in both he and I. Quiet acknowledgment of that personal mission has been my own roadmap for many years. It has served me well and I have every reason to believe it will continue to do so.

Living a Miracle

I fully realize that my way, is not at all the way for everyone, but it has worked remarkably well for me.

I have, for 34 years lived a life of absolute sobriety and looking back now at the journey, I cannot imagine having done it any other way.

Other than a few very fuzzy periods in the mid 1980's, my memories are crystal clear, I literally remember everything. It has been a rich, vibrant and incredible journey, and I can easily replay it in my mind's eye with a clarity that stuns me.

Like everyone else, there have been significant challenges along the way. I have met them however, with a mind clear of distraction, clutter or fatigue. This approach has enabled me to weather life's challenges with full confidence that I will emerge on the other side, safe, whole, and better prepared for the next challenge on my road. That is how it works.

Sobriety earned for me many gifts but perhaps chief among these has been the ability to remain focused and directed at the goals I have set before myself, even goals I set many years ago as a boy. Yes, it has allowed me to successfully navigate some very troubled waters, but it has also allowed me to completely revel in so much of life's joy, not simply in the present, but over and over again. That is what a clear mind is capable of, and it still amazes me.

I suppose this can only truly be understood by those who have lived this way, for an extended period of time. My decision to live a sober life was the smartest thing I have ever done. The result was the rebirth of the young boy who was so filled with marvel and wonder at the world around him.

 That young boy was a whole lot of fun. I nearly lost him at one point, but thank God I didn't, because the life I have led would not have been possible without him.

Chapter Five:

The American Dream

We baby boomers perhaps more than any other generation, came of age at the apex of the American Dream. Even when factoring in the economic and political malaise of the 1970's, the span of our lives saw opportunity and ease of living on a level not previously known and now in retrospect, overlooked and taken for granted. It's not simply nostalgia that causes us to pine for the simpler days and times of little towns like Franklin Massachusetts. There is in fact a growing recognition that those times, even with all of their own difficulties, were indeed unique and special. Social media is replete with postings that fondly recall the days when children played outside, parents took pride in their roles, neighbors were as familiar as relatives, and communities were not 'markets', but more akin to families. People did not move as much, they established deep roots. Generations of families and neighborhoods carried on together. That kind of familiarity necessitated charity amongst people, both economically and socially. Townsfolk knew each other, warts and all, and made allowances because for every blemish known on your neighbor's life, there was one just as apparent on your own. We have forsaken much of that. We all move about at a pace that makes that kind of intimacy impossible, sadly, we seem to prefer it that way. What results then is a colder, less forgiving America. A nation with heightened division, simply because we just don't know each other that well anymore, and we no longer want to bother to. Perhaps the pendulum will swing back, but let's face it, the roadblocks preventing that are pretty formidable. All around us, from the way we work, shop, eat, date, and even worship, the trends is toward further isolation and make believe. I'm certain that the vast majority are completely unaware of these shifting paradigms, but we baby boomers who remember when, are increasingly more forlorn over what we have lost.

A careful examination of this decline from the apex of the 'dream' can be seen within the Catholic education system in our country. While it is sadly very true that the recent scandals within the church, for which I offer no defense, and abhor, have severely diminished the prestige and influence of the Catholic faith in America, the church's slide into irrelevance began long before the scandals broke. A shift in priorities within the highest councils of that church, long ago, in favor of, like everything else in our culture it seems, the 'dark magic' of corporate management and marketing driven nonsense. This is no more apparent than in the abandonment of the real teaching of the faith that was accomplished for generations within the nationwide network of outstanding Catholic elementary schools. Our own little St. Mary's both in Franklin in my youth, and then again in Putnam during my children's time, fell victim to the 'management consultant's buzz saw'. The following letter I wrote to our local bishop, summarizes the event, its impact and my concerns.

Catholic Education in America

To: The most Reverend Bishop Michael R. Cote', Diocese or Norwich CT

Re: A parishioner's thoughts on The Value of Catholic Education in America,

As a 49-year-old Catholic father of three beautiful children and an active member of our small community in northeastern Connecticut, I am very concerned with the current state and valuation of Catholic education in our diocese and country.

I, like many other imperfect men of faith, have faced substantial struggles over the course of my 49 years. Thank God, I have managed to persevere throughout and managed to live a life that roughly corresponds to the convictions of my faith. In this day and age, I consider that a significant accomplishment, a gift from God and a blessing for my family.

Each and every time I have managed to come through one challenge or another, it has occurred to me that perhaps more than anything else, the foundation in faith provided to me by God through his agents, my parents, the good sisters who taught me, and the many priests I have known over the years, is the very thing that allowed me to carry on. Time and time again the lessons both academic and moral, taught to me as a young boy, come back to strengthen and guide me in what is an increasingly dark and threatening world. This realization has only been clarified by my experience as a father, watching my own children and the impact of their Catholic education on their lives. It is further clarified and reinforced by my involvement in our community and the vast disparities in the development of children who have not experienced this blessing. The American culture grows more crass, more materialistic, more anti-faith and simply meaner with each and every passing year. Many would attest that our great nation is in decline, and in the face of the facts, it would be hard to contradict that assessment. I believe that it is no coincidence that America's rise to prominence in the world, its development as the leader in the cause of freedom, charity, and defender of the downtrodden, coincided with the tremendous growth and establishment of a strong Catholic presence in our nation. When the world needed America most, in the time of my parent's youth, during World War Two, the Catholic church was a strong stable and growing part of daily American life, political discourse and most importantly, children's education.

I dare say that the Catholic education of America's youth, particularly that of immigrant Irish, Italian, Poles and others, was a fundamental part of America's meteoric rise to world leadership. In that position of leadership, we American's were able to provide an array of assistance to the world, both spiritual and economic, that has never been seen before in history. This formula, first invoked by the bishop from Baltimore in the 19th century called upon the Catholic faithful to make Catholic schools their first priority, yes even before building a church, build a school.

It was this emphasis on bringing the Gospel to children as the very foundation of their education, that enabled the Roman Catholic Church to survive and blossom in America.

We have lost our way . . . and the effects can be seen everywhere.

The closing of Catholic schools signals the end of Catholicism in America. Denying this, flies in the face of common sense. CCD programs for all the good they attempt can never match a Catholic school in cementing that foundation in faith that our world so desperately and increasingly needs. We close schools that could educate and strengthen a new generation of Catholic leaders, while leaving open and functioning, enormous empty churches that only see activity on Sundays filled with an ever aging population of potential bequests through a will, in hopes of staving off the inevitable financial collapse. Funds are collected and distributed amongst the neediest in our communities, and although this of course is keeping with Christ's call to feed the poor, it is far too often thrown away on people that either do not appreciate it, or have no sense of its origin or meaning. We completely disregard Christ's call to "Make you fishers of men". The true way of charity is not simply to subsidize errors in judgement, but rather to strengthen the faithful that they may be better equipped to lead by example and their own charitable acts to benefit and raise up their own communities. This is best achieved through the establishment of a culture of faith in our youth, without that, we have no future.

The time has come to stop the bleeding, to stop closing schools, to keep them open, not simply as a hope, but as the <u>first priority</u> of our church, <u>first and foremost</u>, bring unto our Lord Jesus Christ, the children!

Surely, I do not have all the facts available to me. The burden and responsibilities facing our current church leaders is simply awesome, and I appreciate that very much.

No doubt they are faced daily with the most difficult decisions, but I sincerely believe that unless the focus is returned to the education of our youth, then our beloved Catholic church in this country will not survive. The time has come to re-establish Catholic education as the FIRST priority of our church. Every dollar should first be earmarked accordingly and when a Catholic education is available and affordable for <u>every</u> Catholic child, then and only then can we afford to offer help to other needs. A drastic measure in the eyes of many I'm sure, but unless we commit ourselves to saving our church this way, we abet its continuing decline and the continuing decline of our nation and world.

Mine is a simple plea, from the limited perspective of a parent who loves his children, worries for their future and for the future of the faith that has so often saved me from ruin. That experience, I believe correlates completely with the experience of history, whereby our nation too has been saved and strengthened by Catholic influence initiated in Catholic elementary schools since the mid-19th century.

I thank you for taking the time to read this missive and beg you to rededicate our diocese and parishes to saving Catholic education in America, for the sake of our youth, our nation, our future and for the Glory of God our father.

Charles F. Harrington

St. Mary of the Visitation Parish and School, Putnam CT

Our time as children, at schools like St. Mary's and in the public-school system as well, were defined by an idealism, patriotism and solid belief in that American dream. We were fully enmeshed in it. Today's detractors have successfully labelled this with a wide variety of negative connotations, but we who lived it, know the truth of it. The education we received, as well as that our parents did before us, along with the recent history and the rise of America as an ideal with worldwide appeal, ignited within us, noble and benevolent passions.

These 'liberal' ideals were best exemplified and most positively impactful through the 1960's and early 70's in very real progress made in the arenas of Civil rights, Women's rights, and a general and intentional inclusion of consideration to our nation's younger people. Whereas the bulk of our nation's history was written and determined it seems by older white men, this time saw a very real and genuine effort at inclusion of ALL peoples of the country, in formulating what kind of nation we would be. This phenomenon was very real and had many substantial beneficial results. It is less important perhaps to recognize that the characterization of the older white men running the entire world was not perfectly accurate.

It could be argued that 'some' older white men were doing so, but certainly the vast majority were simply riding along the trail with the rest of the populace, eking out an existence for themselves and their families, as best they could.

The call at the front of this march toward liberty and social justice was and has been ever since, led by voices very familiar to our generation. The growing divide in our nation, that had not yet really started rolling, would later see the tearing down of these iconic figures, but that was all yet to come. In every Catholic School in America, a photograph of John F. Kennedy was prominently displayed. When the ugly violence of the era took him from us, his younger brothers were called upon to carry the banner of the New Frontier in his place. These were indeed flawed men, like each and every man. Yet I must harken back to my earlier point about how different our world was back then. Our view of our fellow man, cultivated in small, familiar, neighborhoods and towns across America, were colored by a forgiving nature because everyone had their own skeletons, and no one tried to pretend otherwise. It is ironic that in our present-day world that preaches 'tolerance', we have intentionally or not, completely abandoned the concept in reality. I was not immune to all of these influences in my youth. As such as I entered my college years, I had completely bought in to the liberal mantras of the times.

Now make no mistake about it, despite my present day conservative leanings, I still harbor and cherish those classically liberal ideals, bequeathed to me by a nation and culture that enshrined them, not for economic or political gain, as much as for the principles they represented. The following essay reflects my own personal idealism of the time, written after Ted Kennedy's unsuccessful run for President in 1980. I wrote his name in on my ballot, my first Presidential vote. It was only four years later that I would cast my vote again, but this time for the republican candidate Ronald Reagan, and without fully realizing it then, I know now that it was my own initial effort to try and preserve the America I grew up in, and a real belief that Reagan wanted that too.

The Return of Camelot

And an increasing darkness fell upon the land,

so begun with the death of princes.

A fatherless nation, abandoned children,

the image mirrored a generation to come.

Noble purpose, eloquent phrase,

together they fade as light at dusk.

Appointed stewards fulfill their role,

stepfathers offering a facade called home.

Though night had come, they dreamt no more.

But fear not the morrow, the child grows.

The trials of life, it's greatest teachings.

The nation learns, both glad and sad, truths are told.

Their words ring true, and louder still, the ripple grows.

"*We all share the same planet,*

we all breathe the same air,

and we are all mortal."

"*The victims of violence are black and white,*

rich and poor, young and old,

famous and unknown.

They are, most important of all,

human beings whom other human beings loved and needed."

The morning comes, the banner is lifted,

hope and love reborn.

Excalibur freed;

The Dream Never Dies.

The nation's love affair with liberal idealism was nowhere more apparent than in our own home at 18 Anchorage road. My parents, in every sense of the description, were unabashedly liberal democrats and even liberal Catholics, enthusiastic supporters of the 'reforms' within the church initiated through the second Vatican council in Rome. The long-term effects, and frankly, devastating impact of some of those reforms on the church itself, were not yet being realized, though some advocates of a slower moving, conservative church did warn of the dangers. They like others of their ilk in the secular world, were routinely, but somewhat gently nudged aside to make way for the steady march of a self-righteous progress. Woe to today's advocates that might share their hesitance, our new world of 'tolerance' does not so gently allow for them anymore! We were all caught up in those heady days. My older brothers were coming of age, just at the end of the 'hippie' movement. They were 'Jesus freaks', long haired, with Jerusalem cross pendants hanging around their necks. They spent weekends at young Christian encounter groups, organized marches against poverty and hunger and even travelled to Guatemala to witness first-hand the utilization of the charitable funds they raised to help the people of that nation.

My parents enthusiastically supported and encouraged them as they themselves were fully involved in the liberal catholic 'Cursillo' spiritual renewal movement. They were movers and shakers within that movement, even appearing on television talk shows out of Boston to advocate for a more open, inclusive and less rigid catholic faith. The division within our culture though, was underway, we just were so caught up in the euphoric nature of our idealism, that we turned a blind eye to it.

Many years later, upon significant reflection of those times, my mother would make a confession to me about her own naivete. She detailed for me how her self-righteous idealism and the inevitable feeling of moral superiority that came with it, would blind her to the reality of her own human weaknesses. It was for me a startling and deeply impactful lesson. It opened my own eyes wide and was only one of several observations that significantly would alter my convictions. I penned this many years later, on Martin Luther King Day.

Mom Defines Bigotry

Perhaps one of the greatest lessons I learned from my mother was what she taught me about the true nature of bigotry. Growing up in the city of Boston during the time of the then newly developing civil rights movement, followed by the tumultuous times of civil rights marches and real progress of my own youth, my mother witnessed a whole lot of history.

Later as I grew to be a young man, she once shared with me a poignant lesson that she had learned over those years.

'The specific focus of any bigotry does not lessen its ugliness or immorality. There is no one ignorant prejudice that is preferable to another.'

She revealed to me that she herself was raised in a culture, steeped in tradition in Boston especially, but throughout our country's elitist northeast, of disdain and prejudice against southerners and 'rural' folk. Ill-educated, drawl speaking, country bumpkins who desperately needed for their 'betters' to run their lives for them.

She confessed that she too, had once thought that way. She would hear a southern accent and her nose would turn right up, . . . she told me that was very, very wrong. Every bit as wrong as the men standing in front of the college doors in Alabama were. She told me that unbeknownst to her, she was 'taught' to hate, to see 'those' people as less than, as 'others'.

It occurred to her that every image she had seen on television, so much of what she had read and learned had only served to reinforce the stereotypes, and she had fallen 'in-step' with the message. She had in effect, been brainwashed.

Somewhere though, in her heart she knew it was wrong. She was ashamed by that thinking.

I was stunned by her confession, and by the very plain truth of it. I have carried that lesson with me ever since.

Ours is a nation founded upon and made great first and foremost, by the sanctity of the rights and consideration of the individual, . . . over the mob.

Unbridled bigotry is once again rearing its ugly head in this country, but as is so often the case, it comes in disguise and is rarely recognized for what it really is, Ignorance.

It is best served by the righteous mob hell bent on 'defending' themselves against all that they despise.

Fueled by fear, its greatest weapon is subjugation of independent thinking, reaction-ism and frenzy are its sure and stealthy allies.

Until such time as we return to focus on the individual, and protection of the liberty of ONE, we will never have true freedom or peace. Beware as well, because the mob turns quickly, . . .

Bigotry comes in a wide variety of forms and we could all use a good look in the mirror now and then to guard against it.

A lesson taught to me by my mother, appropriately shared today, Martin Luther King Day, It is a lesson worth remembering.

That essay, written years ago, seems almost prophetic when viewed alongside the current state of our national political discourse. Doctor King's sincere appeal to judge NOT by the color of skin, but on the content of character, has been wholly discarded. This is most shocking when we realize that the folks on the supposed liberal side, are the very ones who have so callously dismissed the most important part of his plea, ... the content of character. That concept, of higher character, no longer seems to matter to us as a people. Though we will jump up and down about a particular politician's moral trespasses, we will do so ONLY if he is NOT on our side. The man or woman on our side, will be unassailable, and not subject to such scrutiny, at all.

Instead of focusing on character, an all too uncomfortable concept to a self-absorbed populace, we measure everything ONLY on race and or group identity, being American, or even a neighbor is at best, a secondary consideration. This is nothing short of a complete reversal of the original intentions of those ideal driven, well meaning, liberal thinkers and doers of the previous generations!

<u>Sunset on America?</u>

It is called 'Independence day' for a very good reason, and to say it is merely a celebration of achieving 'independence' from the King of England would be a serious understatement.

The Fourth of July marks Independence Day for ALL Americans. On this day each summer, we celebrate OUR independence, our freedom, our liberation from tyranny of ANY and ALL sorts. We honor the 'Liberty' that is an inherent right, granted by God, NOT benevolently by ANY government or official. We celebrate our BIRTHRIGHT as FREE Americans.

This is the principle upon which our entire nation and its history is based. In America, the rights and freedoms of the INDIVIDUAL CITIZEN take precedence over ALL others, That IS the basis of our great American experiment.

That principle is the basis and foundation of all of our 'civil rights', our 'Women's rights, our Workers, Gay, Disabled, or Human rights. ALL of these and yes, the rights of the unborn as well, are predicated on the uniquely American concept of INDIVIDUAL LIBERTY.

The Constitutional recognition that first and foremost, we, as individuals have the sacred right to determine our own destiny, to conduct our own affairs, and to pursue our own dreams.

The ONLY limitation imposed upon our personal liberty, is the line we shall not cross to impede or deny that very same right to another. No matter how well intentioned, it is not within our rights to determine how best another should conduct THEIR life, for that power must lie ONLY with them.

Somewhere along the way we have forgotten all of this. We have lost our understanding of what 'Liberty' and 'Freedom' mean, and more importantly, what they require of us in the way of protecting them.

They require that we recognize and fully acknowledge those very same rights for others, for without that recognition, none of our own rights are worth a damn!

Over the course of the last 50 years we have been transformed. What was at the end of WWII, a nation of Americans united in the pursuit of a better tomorrow has degenerated into a squabbling mass of competing mobs scrambling, biting and kicking for their own piece of the pie. We have subjugated the time-honored American principle of INDIVIDUAL LIBERTY for mob rule, which is in direct contradiction to the hopes and dreams of all of our ancestors, and our founding fathers AND mothers in particular. Our legislatures and laws were once steadfastly committed to preserving and protecting the rights of INDIVIDUAL citizens AGAINST the tyranny and exploitation of the MAJORITY. Those legislatures now prostitute themselves to whichever group screams loudest and is willing to proffer the most patronage and cash.

Consideration, protection, and aid to 'the little guy', against the threat of the power of the mob is no longer of concern. The 'Rights of Man' have been tossed aside in favor of 'The entitlement of US'.

The great American experiment was for a time, a tremendous success. The concentration of power and authority invested in the INDIVIDUAL citizen, and the protection thereof, built the greatest nation the world has ever seen. Ironically that nation of individuals reached its apex with 'The greatest generation', when American individuals united in self-sacrifice undertook a monumental effort to rid the world of totalitarianism and fascism. Sadly we, their progeny have gone over to the other side, driven by greed, selfishness, sloth and depravity. We have become the monster our forbearers sought to destroy.

Until such time as Americans rediscover and reinvest in the principle of Individual rights and liberties over the instant gratification interests of the mob, we are doomed to enslavement to each and every screeching interest group that next climbs over the backs of ordinary Americans.

The rights and liberties of any civilization are only sacred when they are afforded to the lowliest individual member of that society and are never long secured by the howling of the frantic mob. The entitlements grabbed by each mob are only secure until the next, greedier, louder, more obnoxious mob comes along.

It is time for all of us to wake up. Time to re-educate our children about the core principles upon which this great nation was founded.

It is time to stop joining in the howls of every squabbling 'gimme' group on the evening news and start focusing on individuals in our own neighborhoods.

Time to stop protesting in favor of, or against one 'group' or another and start looking for ways to lend a hand to a single person we meet in any given day.

Time to stop posturing as 'Social Justice Warriors' hell bent on saving the entire world, and instead focus on saying or doing something for an individual stranger we meet on the street, today!

It is time to stop living with our labels, liberal, conservative, democrat, republican, and to start living and acting like Americans, committed to the idea that each of us has the God given right to be who we are, to believe what we believe and to conduct our lives accordingly. If we cannot grasp this very simple, but time honored, proven and inescapable truth, then we shall indeed see the sun set, on this once great and unprecedented AMERICAN experiment in freedom.

Our world, without America and its example, would be a much poorer place to be, and if we are not careful, it will be. God Bless America, and all those who stand by and affirm the high ideals and principles for which she stands.

It is glaringly obvious to anyone paying attention that our current political climate is one of divisive and seemingly hopeless impasse. As Abraham Lincoln so wisely stated, " A house divided against itself, cannot stand".

The most recent presidential election and all of the turmoil associated with it, clearly illustrate this sad state of our nation. It matters less now, which side we are on, but rather, unfortunately, that we are on one or the other. This in my own estimation, is not a natural or blameless situation. It has been fostered by elements in our culture, in our changing values that are increasingly in conflict with those of previous generations. The national news media, once even despite its left leaning slant even then, entrusted to assist us in decision making from a genuinely objective point of view, has abandoned that effort not so much for reasons of either idealism or ideology, but rather in pursuit or the almighty dollar, and the marketing ratings that deliver them. Every headline, every newscast is first run by the marketing departments, overseers of all that is good and necessary in our modern soundbite culture. The end result is a dearth of honest and accurate information and a simple serving of 'red meat' to the desired demographic group. The lowly American individual, he of only a few paltry dollars in his pocket, is completely ignored in favor of the mass market mob, with their collective millions.

The American people, in a stumbling fashion are however catching on. The very popularity of completely unorthodox and arguably fringe candidates illustrates the American people's frustration with our national leader's over reliance upon group think strategy and the mass media's complicit involvement in that approach. They are all operating out of the same Madison Avenue playbook, . . . but the American people are looking to get out of that game.

Bernie and Trump, The People Are Rising

It makes me chuckle to see the media and political establishments going all apocalyptic over the prospect of Bernie being the actual democrat nominee. It was the same with Donald Trump and yet all they have to do to find the real problem is look in the mirror!

I've said it for years now, the MEDIA is the problem folks. The American people are fed up with the lying, staging, the fake stories, the opinion reported as facts. The comfy and cozy relationships, the nepotism, and the 'Elites' telling everyone else in America how and what they should be thinking.

Add to those factors, the way the media works feverishly to pronounce gloom and doom in EVERY broadcast simply to bolster ratings and you get to where we are now. They have lost ALL credibility. Frankly, they are falling victim to their own BS, and it's been a long time coming!

The leading politicians in both parties have been lying to us for years, and the press has been complicit in those lies by repeating them without question for anyone willing to play their 30 second soundbite game. The American people have completely had it.

Bernie's support is the direct result of his speaking directly to the 'little people'. Personally I think many of his ideas are just plain wrong, and go against everything that has made this country the envy of the world. His calling out the elites in both parties though, his call for REAL change and action, resonates very strongly with people who feel both left out, and lied to, by an elite class of politicians and media know-it-alls. Those who constantly talk down to them, take them for granted, and use them simply as mindless ATM machines, sources of cash destined to support their own separate and elite world.

This is what happened with President Trump on the other side, when in his crude but effective manner, he called out the hypocrisy of the GOP. Now it has come home to roost in their own beds for the so-called liberal elites.

Step one to recovery is recognizing there is a problem, and maybe this will force that to happen. Career politicians AND media talking heads both need to get back to basics and recognize that in our American system, they are SERVANTS of the people. Once they start honestly doing the job, we the people employ them to do, then and only then will they be taken seriously once again.

So where does that leave us, we the baby boomer Americans who were raised to love our country and hope and contribute to its betterment for all? I know I am not at all alone in pondering this question. It is a question being asked on both sides of the deeply divided political spectrum. It is driven, for the most part by equal dedication amongst the 'little people' on BOTH sides, to a sincere love of country. This is especially true of those in my generation who were not only taught to love their country, but have so much reason for doing so. It is my earnest hope that we the people can come together and reassert OUR simple values as the driving force in our national discourse.

Flag Day

Each and every morning at school, I remove my hat, place my hand over my heart, and recite the pledge of allegiance. I have often sung the National anthem at local sporting events. I have always loved my country, for nearly 20 years I have flown the flag of The United States of America in my front yard.

The flag isn't up right now, another winter of howling wind (it's always windy here) reduced my flag to tatters, we go through them fairly quickly.

As I gaze at the empty pole in the front yard, I am confronted with my own guilt and sadness when I have to admit that putting that flag back up just doesn't mean as much to me as it used to.

Perhaps it's just cynicism brought on by getting older, or maybe the constant barrage of negativity that we are all subjected to every day, but this just doesn't feel like the America I grew up in, and certainly not the one my parents knew.

Patriotism is passé, we have no leadership, not morally, not politically and certainly not in government.

What we do have is selfishness, greed, violence, anger, rampant materialism, incredibly exaggerated sense of entitlement, envy and jealousy of success.

We have intolerance run amok of anything outside the deemed politically correct, disdain for Faith in God, trivialization and ridicule of traditional family values, and total adherence to moral relativism, nothing is really wrong, everything is ok as long as I get to do my thing . . .

And for those of you who think I am simply a raving right-winger, I would remind you that one of my chief personal heroes is Robert F. Kennedy. I have a picture of him on the wall in my office at home. I wonder what this devout Catholic, father of 11, ruthless pursuer of organized crime, staunch defender of civil rights, cold warrior turned anti-Vietnam war candidate, and great American, would think of his country today? If my own read on him is correct, I am afraid that he might find himself in the same situation I am, worried for his children's future and looking at an empty flagpole and wondering, why bother???

It has been my purposeful intent to try to make this book as 'a-political' as possible. Those that know me well would marvel at that endeavor. I have always had an ear for politics, studied it in college and was schooled in it by my father who was a 'clean for Gene McCarthy', democrat way back in 1968, when I was a 7 year old boy. We had a conversation at that time, on one of our many Saturday morning trips to the town dump.

Discussing the coming election of 1968, dad asked me who I thought should be President. Mind you, I was seven years old, but this is exactly what my dad would do with me. We had innumerable conversations that one would assume, were well beyond my tender years. I confidently asserted to dad, that Hubert Horatio Humphrey was the right man for the job. I know for certain that he was tickled that I did not choose his guy, McCarthy. Independent thinking was afoot here, and that is what dad wanted. The truth of the matter is, that to my seven-year old ears, what could sound more presidential than 'Hubert Horatio Humphrey'. Whatever imaginative dialogue I threw at him to justify my endorsement was irrelevant.

He seemed very pleased with my assessment and I have been thinking for myself ever since. I have placed myself on virtually every side of the political spectrum over the years, from the over-zealous and idealistic liberalism of my youth, all the way to the curmudgeonly conservatism of these my older years. The fact is however, despite the protestations and even condemnations of those who have foolishly debated me, I have retained elements of all of it in my core. There remains a bit of the hippie, with a healthy dose of rabid Goldwater libertarianism running through all of my veins.

Chapter Six:
Loss and Sorrows

Now that I've covered the American dream, or nightmare depending upon the reader's own perspective, certainly no less valid than my own, let's get any other unpleasantries out of the way. It is an inescapable fact of life that the older we get, the more heartache and loss we must endure. That is just the way it is.

On the one hand we can be grateful for all of the blessing we have enjoyed, but hand in hand with them comes the tragedies and loss that impact all of us. The following chapter seeks to touch upon those losses, as seen through my own tear-filled eyes.

It is my hope not to depress or even sadden the reader, but rather to share in our mutual grief in hopes of delivering some solace and comfort to all of us, stricken with the passing of our loved ones. We have all suffered these losses, and in the immediate aftermath we are overwhelmed with grief and struggle to find meaning in death.

Perhaps after some time, if we pause and carefully reflect, the meaning will be found not in the passing of those we loved, but rather in their living, and the eternal blessing their lives had, on our own.

God Needs Angels

In memory: Maryjane Harrington 7/21/64 – 7/20/06

Webster's dictionary defines angels as messengers of inspiration from God.

God needs angels.

We all need angels.

Maryjane was in life the most selfless among us.

Her capacity to Love was extraordinary, and dare I say, otherworldly.

It seems to some of us that her entire life was a struggle, yet she lived it always with a smile and a selflessness that was simply remarkable.

She was first and foremost a loving mother.

She was our smiling sister,

She was your gentle friend.

She was tireless in her work,

Perseverance and courage were her shields.

At 19 years old, she became a mother.

Relying solely on the great love within her

She raised her son in a fashion we should all aspire to.

The result of her life's work,

is completely evident in the fine young man that our Patrick has become.

She is now at peace, it is we who suffer her loss.

I am absolutely certain she is with God in Heaven.

God needs Angels

We all need angels.

She will no doubt watch over each and every one of us.

She will do so with the same selfless love and tireless effort that she demonstrated throughout her short life.

It is most fitting to consider Angels today.

Maryjane was an angel on earth,

and now with a beautiful set of red feathery wings

she will do God's work and watch over each and every one of us from above.

We who are left behind, are of course heartbroken.

We can however take some small solace in faith that our beloved angel is at peace with God

She is destined to continue her message of inspiration.

This is the work of angels,

A task our Janie is perfectly suited for.

May she forever rest in peace and watch over us all.

In these most difficult times of loss and mourning, we often struggle to even remember the living. Inevitably the task of leading family and friends through the crisis falls to one or a few brave members of the family or community. Their words and actions inexorably seem to fit both the occasion and the spirit of those we have surrendered to God. I have been thrust into this role on more than one occasion and thus am particularly sensitive to its honor, and its burdens. In each of our families and communities, we have leaned heavily on individuals who carried us through this torment. They often remind us of all that was good and admirable, and loved, about the deceased. We are indeed comforted by their words, but who then will comfort them?

Remembering the Living

Dear Richard,

I wanted to take a moment, during this most difficult time to write you this letter. I want to write down and try to express to you my very deep love and gratitude for all that you have done and all that you are, to me and everyone else in our family. It is no surprise that you have been our rock. This has always been the case. I have said it before and still firmly believe that no little boy ever had a better big brother. I am not alone in my sentiments either.

Maryjane adored you, with good reason. I believe very strongly that she is with God in heaven. In heaven she is smiling warmly as she watches you do what you have done so well for so many years. She knew in life, and she knows now that her big brother Richard could be counted upon. She like me, made many conscious decisions in life based on careful observation of a role model we loved, our brother Richard.

When she, or I, tried to be clever, when we aimed toward integrity and doing the right thing, when we needed to be strong, when we were parenting to the best of our ability. When we showed compassion for the little guys in this world, when we undertook any athletic endeavor and strived to do our very best, we did all of these things with your example foremost in our minds.

I know very well the extent of your capacity to love. That tremendous heart comes with a price, a deep sensitivity and empathy for others that can cut very deep. It is because I know this that my heart aches so deeply for you. I can only offer my prayers and continuing love in that regard.

You have done all of us, and especially Maryjane and Patrick a great service throughout this ordeal.

Dad would be enormously proud of you, as would Grandpa Moore.

Know and never forget, I have always loved you with all of my heart, like no other, and I always will.

Charlie

My own losses by any account, have been too many. That I suppose comes with the risk of being from such a large family, that has in turn been blessed with a crowd of beloved friends and relatives that are near and dear, but ultimately will also pass on. Among the many losses I have experienced, three in particular stand out among them.

They stand out because they were not 'family' so to speak, but friends. Family members of course hold amongst the most special and cherished places in our hearts, but true friends who earn that same status and appreciation, are an unexpected pleasure. Yes, we expect particular loved ones to pass on, such is the relentless march of time.

When a friend dies however, especially by all accounts too soon, those losses it seems we are less likely to be prepared for, and thus the pain all the deeper. These memories I share here are my own of course, but the hope is that within them, readers will recognize the love and longing for those close to them, no longer physically here, but now and forevermore, only so in spirit

Artie Whitmore

I first met Artie almost 40 years ago, but I remember it very well. I played soccer in the Franklin town league with my brother Dave. Artie was the goalie on our team and my brother David was on another team coached by Artie's Dad, Bruce.

He was two years older than I, and from the very beginning I thought he was "cool".

He wore a red headband to keep his long hair out of his face on the soccer field, and big red kneepads, to protect him in his fearless assaults on anyone that got near his goal. Bruce's team, with David, won the league championship that year, we were the second-place team. We really weren't that good, but because we had the best goalie in the league, we were able to stay on the field with them. It was my first year playing, I was tiny and skinny and not very good, but Artie took me under his wing and taught me to play.

He immediately earned my admiration and affection, and the nature of that relationship never changed.

When I visited and said good-bye to him last week, he said to me as I was leaving the room. "Ok Kid, take care of yourself" That's how he talked to me, and I remember he used to call me 'kid' all those many years ago on the soccer field, "don't worry kid, you'll get it", amazing!

David and Artie developed a friendship that rivaled brotherhood. They were inseparable through their teenage years. Artie's younger brother Stephen and I simply flittered around these two older, obviously cooler guys. Those were very interesting times as they are in any teenager's life.

As we got older, we became closer. Our social circle was solidifying in a manner that amazingly has held together for all these years. In our twenties, Artie, always the responsible one, was the first to actually buy and own his own place, and we, a great bunch of us, moved in every weekend to party together, watch football and enjoy ribs and hot wings that Artie would cook on his hibachi.

Many of us worked together at the Middlesex news, and at lunch we would make the quick trip to the package store for a beer, (always just one for Artie), and to that Rib restaurant whose name escapes me now. There were also scratch tickets to buy, and then back to work on the three-knife trimmer at the news.

We played a lot of golf at Millwood farms, only 14 short holes so you could play the entire course after a day at the news, before heading up to Bill's package store where Artie worked the counter and I either sat around, or stocked the shelves.

I had some dark days about that time, and my friend Artie helped carry me through them. When I say carry, that's what I mean. I lived with he and Brenda for a time, because frankly I had nowhere else to go. They took me in, and never asked for anything in return, and on those few occasions where I was able to offer something, he would flatly refuse it. We who knew and loved Artie, know full well that his friendship was given unconditionally.

In all the years I have known him, I never once saw him be unkind to anyone. The closest I can remember is when he might get upset with Stephen or I at the house on Skyline Drive for doing something stupid. Again, he was always the responsible one, looking out for many of us to make sure we didn't do something stupid.

I remember very well his presence in that home on Skyline drive. It was like having an additional parent around, but make no mistake about it, his approach was always kindly and probably more patient than it should have been. He was clearly in charge however, and we knew it and were perfectly ok with it, all of us.

I remember when Artie took the name Whitmore. We talked about it. It was in his mind, "the right thing to do". He was deeply appreciative of Bruce and Eleanor and changing his name was his testament to that fact. He was proud of them, and proud of who they had helped him become, and the changing of his name was his way of saying so. That very act itself maybe sums up who he was in many ways.

I met him as Artie Eastman, cool, part Indian kid who was really good at soccer and the girls all loved him.

I watched him become Artie Whitmore, a modern-day Indian Brave, like the heroes of his beloved Louis L'Amour western novels. Humble and stoic but filled with compassion and a sense of justice that few men are blessed with. Kind and patient almost to a fault, fair and dependable, hardworking and yet quick to smile.

My friend Johnny said it well when he thought out loud of telling folks that a good friend had passed away, "yea he was a really nice guy" a simple statement, often heard, but think about it in this particular case, No . . .really, this really was a nice guy.

I am unabashedly a man of faith, I am not at all shy about that. As a man of faith I told Artie last week that his work was not done. He had lived a life of powerful example to so many of us, but yet that work is not done.

People like Artie, and they are few, who leave us long before we are ready to let them go, are destined to continue to work on our behalf from another realm. This I have to believe because nothing else makes any sense.

From the time I met him, Artie reminded me of Jesus Christ. I dare say that I am not the only one that had that impression. As kids it was more perhaps his physical appearance, with his straight flowing hair, but I think perhaps even then it was more than that. It was his kindness and gentleness. The great irony is that now so many years later, as I ponder Artie's place in my life, and the lives of all of us who loved him I realize that indeed he did, and should have, reminded us of Jesus Christ, because he lived his live in a manner that certainly can be called Christian. Yet he did it without obvious intent, perhaps it seemed effortless to us, but not without effort. Ultimately, he did it unconditionally.

We are blessed to have known and loved him, and I for one pray to God that the lessons his life offers are not lost upon me. When I was a boy I wanted to be cool like him, as a man I hope to remember his kindness, patience, and warmth so that I might incorporate some of that into my own life and the lives of people around me.

We thank you Artie for being our friend, I have no doubt that God will bless and Keep you and I trust you will watch over each and every one of us for the remainder of our days.

Rest in Peace . . . Kid

Brian Woodman

Good morning friends. Devin, I think I can safely speak for all of us here in thanking you for arranging this service. So many of us were unable to get to VT for the funeral and we are grateful for this opportunity to show our love for Brian.

Given what I know about him, this is exactly what he would have done under these circumstances, no doubt your father is both pleased and very proud of you today. Thank you.

Once again, we are called together, sharing our loss and condolences at the departure of a lifelong and dear friend. When Brent asked me to convey my thoughts to all of you, I was prepared and more than willing. Brian was a very good friend to me for nearly 40 years and frankly I honestly believe he would expect me to be standing here. Brian never once said no to me . . . how then, could I possibly say no now.

We all have our roles in life, part of mine it seems, is to try to write the story of our life and love together on all of our hearts. This is my obligation, I have embraced it, and I offer this small effort in gratitude for all that has been given to me by so many of you. I speak even for those of you who do not know me but have enjoyed the benefit of close friendships and the many blessings that come along with them, so often not fully recognized until a day like today comes along.

I told our friend Mac, "Woody was a funny duck". He laughed and said, "aren't we all?" "Amen" Mac, aren't we all?

Brian and I worked together for many years, The Middlesex News, Boston Offset/USA today and Worcester County Newspapers. How many of us learned to work, began our work, with the Woodmans? Our love and deepest sympathy is extended to them, a beautiful family that has endured too much, but has done so in an exemplary and courageous manner. Our prayers and sympathies are also extended to Brian's wife and his children. Although I do not know each of them well, their pictures have been on my kitchen wall every Christmas for many years. I did know their father very well, and I know he loved his family very, very much.

   This is not the first time I have spoken in remembrance of a dear friend, and I know too well it may not be the last. Each passing though, teaches me, and us, a little more about how to live.

As kids growing up in Franklin, we never gave much thought to qualities such as dignity or grace. When we did consider courage, it was in the context of facing down a slapshot or climbing the highest tree. However, a lifetime of living and watching each other grow and encounter life's challenges sure does alter our perspectives.

Brian's life is a good example of that. I don't think his life was <u>ever</u> easy, I think maybe it was <u>always</u> more difficult and challenging than he let on. Aside from the lifelong friendship and work together, Brian and I shared battles with many of the same demons. He fought those battles courageously. His life was never easy. Perhaps that is why he was able to finish it with such grace and dignity. Living his life, forged in him a steely courage that enabled him to carry this battle to the end, almost with nonchalance, and this lightened the load for those who loved him. That of course was Brian's way, if he could do something for you,.. he did it,.. without a thought or hesitation. He never counted or measured his contributions, it's as if he never considered 'no' as an option.

I spoke with him two weeks ago, he was of course gravely ill, I told him I was coming over to borrow some money for gas and cigarettes . . without missing a beat he said "how much do you need Charlie?, c'mon over ". Then he paused,.. thought for a moment,.. probably smiled,.. and said, "should I come by and pick you up?" We were having fun with that, but I know that there was, within his quips, a hint of pride, some peace, and more than a hint of love. You see, joking like that, reminiscing like that reminded <u>both of us</u> of the best parts of <u>him</u>. That is part of the lesson of his life. We are told that when we give unselfishly to others, we will reap benefits tenfold. The tenfold benefits though are not to be measured in material ways. The benefit truly is in Grace and Blessing that can only be felt and measured in our own hearts,.. ... the trick is to allow ourselves to feel them! Throughout his life Brian gave unselfishly to others. In the end he received,.. and I believe continues to receive,.. his tenfold reward. I believe he knew that, he felt it, and he did what he could even then, to share it with those he loved, and those who loved him.

This is precisely why he was able to finish his fight the way he did, a lifetime of little givings had earned him grace and strength few of us could muster.

His faith was strong, my mother was his catechism teacher when he went through the process of receiving his Catholic Confirmation as an adult. Whenever we spoke, he asked for her, he had grown close to her at that time, and I was sure to tell her recently his faith remained strong right to the end. Though many of us knew Brian for many, many years, there were parts of him that he kept very private and to himself and his faith was one of them. I was fortunate that he did reveal a good portion of that part of himself to me and I can attest that his faith was indeed strong and a great comfort to him to the end. Again, the opportunity to learn is here. His quiet faith and his private relationship with God, present to me a model, and example to follow. His confidence in that rapport with his 'higher power' allowed him to find peace and to be at peace with <u>exactly</u> who he was, and that is a huge blessing for anyone.

We, . . his friends, . .are a very big extended family. So many of us continuing to be a presence in each other's lives, sometimes more, sometimes less, but always present in some extent. Sadly there are more funerals than baptisms, but the opportunity to love and care for one another has never been greater.. .I believe Brian would very much want all of us to realize that. We are indeed funny ducks like him. Like him, each of us is incredibly unique. We honor his memory each time we embrace one another, having known each other so long, having learned so much together and apart. When we think of one another and smile, feeling that inner peace, knowing that just being each other's friends is indeed good enough, satisfying enough, and in the end, one of life's truest treasures, it is then that we will be enjoying the tenfold benefit of grace that our friend Brian has shown us. May he rest in peace and may the good Lord forever hold him, gently, in the palm of his hand.

Susan Hurd Healy

It was her smile, her gentle, caring and so very sincere smile, that got me every time.

Both her parents and her sisters share that same serene and beautiful smile.

Whenever I saw her, I was greeted with and touched by that smile. There was just a hint of her thinking, 'your silly Charlie' in her grin, . . . but more than anything else there was a warm, welcoming and genuine affection in that smile.

How do some people smile so beautifully when life can be so difficult?

There was real joy within her, and that must be why.

Susan was a courageous woman, her life, though filled with many, many joys and blessings, also had more than its share of challenges.

I knew her for more than 40 years and never once, not once, did I ever hear her complain.

When she and Mark got married, and moved into that little apartment on Pleasant street, I thought it a good idea to 'kind of move in' with them, for about a month if I remember correctly.

They were NEWLYWEDS!!!

She did not complain.

When we all vacationed together on the cape, we boys spent virtually all of our time and energy being complete knuckleheads.

Susan made sure we ate, got some sleep, and stayed out of jail,

And she never complained.

She got a little mad at me once. Well, maybe a lot mad, . .

Driving to reach the ferry for a day trip to the vineyard during one of our summer vacations, I was impatient with the bumper to bumper traffic and decided the other lane of the highway would be quicker.

She was sitting right next to me with Mark, in the front seat of my old Buick. She was terrified, and I still feel guilty about that.

She forgave me though. She would just add that incident to others that were part of why there was always a little 'Silly Charlie' in her smile.

I get that in the smiles from all of these Hurds, and somehow it tickles me. I am much more than just comfortable with it.

Dick and Albie looked at me the same way. Somehow, they all have a way of seeing right inside to your very soul and seeing something good there. I guess that is why she and they, can and do smile the way they do, even in the face of life's difficulties.

My two oldest friends married these sisters. My friend Brian, God rest his soul, dated a third. All four girls were an integral part of the growing up of that ol' gang of mine.

I marvel at the consistency and commonality of goodness and kindness that they all share. I told Mark on many occasions, I wish there were more Hurd girls, four was just not enough.

Can you imagine Dick rolling his eyes at that thought!!!

Albie though, . . . she would be grinning from ear to ear!

Mark, Scott and I have shared a lifetime together. Each of us knows full well the joys and agonies of each other's journey. Even on a day like today, I don't think any of us would change a thing. We are completed by the lives we have led, the loves we have known and even the pain we have suffered.

When we get down and beat up along the way, we look to the examples of dignity and grace that exist in our world.

My brother Dave pointed out to me recently that "some people just walk on a higher plane".

A simple but profound observation, and so very applicable to this occasion.

It is those people, those that walk on a higher plane, and do so with a dignity, grace and a gentle serenity that can give us the courage and strength to carry on.

This then, is how I will remember this remarkable woman.

She walked on a higher plane. It was my great blessing to walk along with her for some of the way.

My friend Mark knows full well how much I loved her, . . .

from the very beginning, I loved her, as all of you did too.

We loved her forever and will miss her even longer.

Hers will be a much deserved, gentle and beautiful rest, with Albie and Dick, with her nephew Joshua and with all of those whose lives contributed to the development of her own caring soul.

We, here, of course will miss her greatly.

We can and should however, try to take some solace in the knowledge that just as when we were foolish youngsters, . . .Susan will continue to watch over us. She will continue to forgive us and love us, and in our hearts, minds and memories, she will continue to smile at us.

Thank you Susan, for everything.   Rest in Peace.

It is among the greatest ironies that the saddest of stories are those that are too often, never told, . .

Because isn't it truth, that in the telling, very often, great beauty is revealed, . .

We shed heartfelt tears and marvel at the depths of feelings touched, . . .And those very same tears gently wash the sadness away, leaving only of course, the beauty! Go ahead and share the story, . . and we will all share in the beauty.

The following piece was written by my daughter Katherine, ... she really is a wonder, and my book and this chapter would be incomplete without this inclusion. The story here is not one of personal loss, but the emotion included is right on the money, and a reminder to all of us, of the indominable power of the human spirit, the precious value of every human life, ... every, every minute of it.

'Faith'

Faith – a 'Blackout poem' by Katherine Harrington with phrases taken from Elie Wiesel's Pulitzer prize winning novel 'Night'. (page number of selected words and phrases are indicated in parenthesis.) This was an assignment for my freshman English class.

The book was incredibly moving and thought provoking and my impressions were best expressed in this poem.

A copy of this poem was sent to Mr. Wiesel and he responded with a beautiful letter, one of the last he ever wrote just prior to his passing. It is a treasure that I have kept framed and will forever cherish.

Mr. Wiesel's recognition of this work only served to deepen the impact the entire intellectual experience. I am grateful for the opportunity and the lessons assigned in my freshman English class with Ms. Katie Burns at The Woodstock Academy.

Faith

*A hesitant light began to hover on
the horizon (87)*
Hell does not last forever (41)

Hunched over (8)
Eyes cast down (8)
Under (10)
Hostile faces (12)
Hate filled stares (12)

To throw salt on their wounds (11)
An atmosphere of fear and terror (9)

That was all I knew (4)
Tears like drops of wax (7)
Life (7)
Death (7)
It was all in the abstract (9)
Ruled by delusion (12)

A world without God (68)
Without love or mercy (68)
Nothing but ashes (68)
This decay (66)
This misery (66)
Opened the door to death (77)

Faith (41)
A small red flame (86)
Like an injection of morphine (80)
Like a dream in the first hours of dawn (18)
No more fear (12)
No more anguish (12)
By a miracle (6)
To start a new (9)

Hell does not last forever (41)

Night by Elie Wiesel
'Blackout poem' by Katherine Harrington - 2015

Chapter Seven:

Hope for the future

We have traveled quite a bit on this little adventure, from the idyllic green fields of the west of Ireland 150 years ago, through the end of the baby boom and their coming of age, all the way to the present day. Where does that leave us, and where do we go from here? My family roots in education and the high value that was placed upon it, suggest a logical course. In my own work in academia, I have witnessed first-hand the benefits and impact of learning, and all it can do to enhance not only each individual life, but communities as whole. I think then it might be fair and accurate that our way forward will rely at least in significant measure, on our collective ability to keep on learning. This is not as simple as obtaining more schooling, more advanced degrees or learning new math. When I speak of 'learning' my intent covers a much wider spectrum than just schooling. In our current culture, schooling specifically is coming under some pretty harsh, and wholly justified in my mind, criticism.

My father's insistence on critical and independent thinking would not necessarily sit well in the storied halls of many of our nation's centers for higher learning. Too often nowadays, the schooling is restricted to only what is deemed acceptable to the powers that be, and that friends is the very antithesis of true learning. There's an old expression, I'm not sure who first coined it, "I've learned more from those I disagreed with, than those with whom I agreed." That is a simple, but rather profound statement that for me, defines true learning. If we stifle dissent and disagreement, even in the name of 'social justice' aren't we risking the stifling of all learning as well?
If Galileo had strictly followed the proscriptions of the Vatican in his day, how much longer would it have taken for us to learn the many things his critical thinking revealed?

I know I am not the first to point out this danger, but it is worth repeating because my own experience in American Academia, both at the secondary and university level, has clearly demonstrated to me that we are on the precipice of a dark age when it comes to learning. Today's rabid enforcement of political correctness is every bit as tyrannical and closed minded, as was the Vatican's back in Galileo's day. That kind of restrictive thinking has little to do with progress or justice but is based first and foremost in power and absolutism, two things that when combined, pose a very frightening threat indeed.

Chasing Wisdom

I always wondered about the deepening faith of older folks. In doing so I assumed, as so many have, that this was a natural development of people faced with their own mortality. I remain certain that is true for a good number of people, but there is also I believe, another factor.
I think particularly in our modern culture, we often operate under the mistaken assumption that our 'maturation' process into 'adulthood' comes to some kind of conclusion as we traverse our twenties. Late bloomers like myself, might even extend that into the thirties, but surely our growing is done by then right???. . . I don't think so.

In fact, it may very well be, for many, that the real growth only occurs much later than we supposed. The unrelenting stimulus of life bombards us in our earliest years, filling up the empty sponge that is our mind and soul. People have remarked forever it seems, on those very early critical years. Are they infancy through five, through ten, even into adolescence?
What if that unbridled assault on our blank slate and its accompanying confusion, continues much, much longer?
What if the apparent serenity and calm that we often observe in our elderly is the actual indicator that the bombardment has finally ceased, or at least slowed to a point where stock can be taken, and a place found in the world to peacefully exist?

We so very often take our elderly for granted. If we are paying close attention though, we can notice something. It may simply be a slight twinkle in the eye, or an upturn at the corner of a grin that denotes an inside view, one we have not yet attained. Perhaps older folks are not quite as concerned with their own mortality as we thought.

Perhaps they simply see things clearer than we do, bereft of the cacophony of noise that our busy lives drown us with.

This possibility might give us pause. Perhaps we would do well to consider the old expression, "when I was 18, I could not believe how dumb my parents were, and at 28, I could not believe how much they had learned in 10 years!" Maybe, just maybe, Wisdom is the goal?

And how is wisdom obtained? It comes of course from experience and there is no shortcut for that. There is though, one sure fire aide in traveling the road to wisdom, and I think that is awareness. If we pay very close attention, practice sincere reflection from a perspective rooted in humility, then our journey along life's road to wisdom might in fact gain both direction, and acceleration.

Stop and think folks, it may be as simple as that. That may be why the old fellow or lady smiles so serenely.

Much like it was with my father before me, education and learning were placed very high on the priority list in my own children's experience. The results speak for themselves. They were, and two still are, outstanding students. Each earned a bevy of academic honors in their school days, and each has continued to demonstrate a love of learning that would absolutely make my own dad very proud, of that I am most certain. When my eldest son William graduated from high school, I was working as a campus security officer at the school. The graduating class of 2014 selected me as their Commencement ceremony's Baccalaureate speaker. It was one of the greatest honors of my life. Commencement day just so happened to also be 'Father's Day' that year, and I can honestly say it was the best Father's Day gift I ever received. I delivered the following speech to my friends, the 2014 graduating class of The Woodstock Academy.

Class of 2014 – Commencement Speech

Ladies and Gentlemen, Mr. Sanford, Mrs. Singleton, Members of the board, distinguished guests, members of the faculty, Parents, . . . and my friends, . members of the Woodstock Academy class of 2014.

Once again we find ourselves in a situation where the question on everyone's mind might very well be, Whose bright idea was it, to give this guy a microphone?, AGAIN!!!

Well you all did, and I am honored, grateful and humbled by your decision.

We started here together when you were freshmen. My first year at the Academy. Quite a few of you I have known much longer, some knew me as "Coach Charlie" and some met me when they were in kindergarten. It has been my distinct pleasure to see so many of you grow up, to mature and develop into the kind of people that give me reason to smile and give me hope and optimism in the face of all the dire forecasts the world throws at us every day.

I have been called upon here to deliver a message of inspiration, . .

It is in fact, YOU, who inspire me.

As graduates, you enter now a world fraught with crisis,

Global warming, rising oceans, imminent meteor strikes, economic recessions and depressions, civil unrest, religious apostasy, political hypocrisy, weekly storms of the century, global cooling, climate change, fracking and earthquakes, hate crimes, a new cold war, the list of impending doom is unending and relentless, Just read the paper or watch an hour of two of doom and gloom news media, we are all in VERY big trouble!

I have news for you, it was no different when I graduated high school in 1978. We had runaway inflation, air pollution, the population explosion, the coming ice age, the original cold war, the oil crisis and the rest of our own list of impending disasters.

We survived, . . and so will you.

And yet. faced with all this doom and gloom you choose the little happy old guy with a smile on his face, to be your inspirational speaker. Haven't any of you been paying attention????

How can you possibly prepare for all that lies ahead with only the questionable wisdom of a man whose sanity more than a few have wondered about?

Your selecting me to be your inspirational speaker is flattering, and much appreciated, but perhaps it says more about you, than me.

Perhaps because of who YOU all are, because of the kind of people YOU are, because of the ways in which YOU were raised, the values YOU hold dear and the way YOU would all like to see the world be,

Perhaps we are not really doomed to a made for television, disaster movie, future! Just in case you didn't think I've been paying attention these last few years, I have. I've watched, and listened, and witnessed, and most of all, I've smiled!

I have been fortunate to witness your kindness, compassion and optimism. I've watched and admired your growing friendships. I've seen great acts of courage and determination both on the athletic fields, in the classrooms and in the music halls at this school. Anyone with my point of view, . .and just like at basketball games, . . I've had the best seat in the house, . . seeing you all from where I sit, it would be difficult NOT to be optimistic about our collective future.

Perhaps most of all, I've seen your courage, in many little things each and every day. Courage is the human trait I find most admirable and as such, I am keen to notice it, even in everyday situations.

When you get to my age, and especially when you have children of your own, you come to realize just how much courage growing up requires.

Courage – Little if anything in life can be accomplished without it, It takes courage to live life to the fullest, . . to love, to laugh, to cry, to mourn, . . all require great courage.

It takes courage to be who you are, . . . to find out who you are. . .It will require courage to face mistakes, and there will be mistakes. . . . You'll need courage to learn from them. To put one foot in front of the other and to carry on.

The good news is that you have already done this a gazillion times, you just may not realize it yet. If you think hard though, remember back to freshman year, or middle school, I'm certain that each and every one of you has had to muster great courage on several occasions.

The circumstances are as unique as your fingerprints, but the commonality is in the requirement, you have ALL had to overcome, and you have done so, brilliantly!

Where is my friend Taylor Butts? . Taylor played football for me when she was 10 years old, the only girl on the field, think that was scary? and yet she may have been the bravest player on our team, now she is a grown woman hard working and responsible, who I would bet on in any situation

John McGinn, from kindergarten on he has endured my pestering, it took a couple years to become my pal, and I'm glad he had the courage to finally acknowledge that crazy guy who said hello to him every morning at St. Mary's.

Austin Stone singing the National Anthem, . . just the way it is supposed to be sung,   He only looks fully composed, cool and collected, he gets nervous just like the rest of us, isn't that true Austin?

Will Bourgeois, the very first pal of Billy's to come over to our house at 5 years old, never said one word to me through the entire visit, . . a look of complete bewilderment in his eyes.

I've watched him grow and mature, facing adversity with great courage, and setting an example everyone can follow.

Jordan Adams singing 'Loch Lommond" for his football teammates. Think that took courage?

Cheerleaders Jenna Clinton and Mariel Baker – One at the anchor, the other at the apex, out on the floor for every game, and especially at every difficult football game, never once letting up in their enthusiasm and support.

Chris Lowry – his unselfish play, doing everything he could to make everyone around him excel.

It is never easy to be in the spotlight, especially when it shines on you from freshman year on. To fight your natural instincts to "take it to the rim" and instead look for opportunities to help others shine, that takes courage.

My friend Trent Peters. Obviously I was always 'the little guy', I've watched Trent play ball since 5th grade, always with tenacity and courage and always against much bigger players, this year he gets to Five foot ten, . . . and plays like he's Six Foot Three! . . . How proud do you think I am of him?

Gymnasts Courtney Osborn and Bree Hussong, such poise and grace, not just 4-year varsity, but four year Champions. Good Lord the balance beam, I am scared just walking by one!!! Pressure?, what pressure?

And how about Big Tim Davis – what a story there!

Kaulman Lengyl, from 5 years old I have watched you grow, . . and grow! Courage?

Kaulman wants to run into burning buildings and save lives, my dad was also a firefighter, among the noblest of professions.

Or Duane Tao, Kent Kamanzi, and April Zhu, and the rest of our international students, who came halfway around the world from countries far away to us here in Woodstock, like the many immigrants to this country who left home at young ages, to begin anew in America, that courage built this country, and ours is a better world because of the courage of people like them..

And of course, my very own Billy. I did ask him if it was ok for me to come to work here, he rolled his eyes and agreed, telling me he was 'used to me' by now.

Week in, week out on that football field, . . . against incredible odds, under the microscope as quarterback, with every opposing player gunning for him, Then on Monday after another very difficult game, he's back on that practice field, leading and encouraging his teammates, setting the example, determined to once more, give it everything he had.

His courage and effort were nothing short of amazing and made his father, very, very proud.

And all of you unnamed here, who quietly made this journey, . . . many who allowed me to befriend them along the way, . . that too, took courage.

And there are many more, too many to cover here today, all those presentations in class, asking someone for a date, helping someone out, the list is endless. There have been so many victories and accomplishments.

When you think life is getting the better of you, remember, . . remember how much you've faced and overcome in the past. Doing well in the first job interview isn't really any different than facing all the new kids on the first day at a new school, only the circumstances are different.

The kid who made it through that first day is the same person who will get through that interview, or bounce back after losing a job, or find happiness in a new relationship. You have conquered before and there is no reason to believe you can't conquer some more!

You have been well prepared, I know a great many of your families, they have done their part. Woodstock Academy is a terrific school, and you will realize that more and more the further away from here you get, I promise you that. You've had great teachers so many of whom genuinely care and invest themselves in your future, that too you will see with greater and greater clarity as time marches on.

So, what happens going forward is up to you. What will you do with all you have been given? With three quarters of the people in this world eating rice out of a bowl twice a day for nourishment, no matter how difficult your own journey might have been to this point, so very many would trade places with you in a minute. Don't take it for granted. You have been set up and prepared to lead, . . to help, . . to be admired, . . and to SERVE, and that is indeed an honorable position to be in. What will you do with the opportunity?

The one and only place to start the future is with ourselves and the only advice I can really give is the same advice my own father gave me over 40 years ago. He was a schoolteacher, father of nine children, and my own personal hero and source of inspiration, still to this day! Way back in 1971, I was a red headed, freckle faced, 10-year-old boy. My Dad was my hero, and I made it a point each day to get out of bed early, ahead of my brothers and sisters so that I could steal some time alone with him. I remember one particular morning; I was helping to make oatmeal in a huge pot for my 8 brothers and sisters. The morning's Boston Globe was on the kitchen table, the big story was about a tremendous Tsunami, (we called them "Tidal waves", back then), that had hit the country of East Pakistan, now known as Bangladesh. Nearly 200 thousand lives were lost, a monumental human tragedy.

On the front page of the paper was a big picture of a young Pakistani boy, close to my own age at the time. He was obviously malnourished, ribs showing and a distended belly, an empty bowl in his hand. In the gray of this picture the thing that jumped out most, was the bright white smile on the boy's face.

My father pointed to it and asked me, "Charlie, with all the horrible things going on around him, how could that little boy possibly be smiling??? I gave him a perfectly appropriate 10-year old's answer. "Maybe he knows his picture is going to be in the paper". My dad smiled and said, maybe that's it, or maybe he is smiling because HE CHOOSES TO BE HAPPY! Dad then carefully explained to me that each and every day of our lives we will have a choice.

We can choose to be Happy, or we can choose to be miserable.

<u>Regardless of the circumstances</u>, WE ALWAYS HAVE THAT CHOICE.

Around the world there are plenty of millionaires who choose to be miserable, and they are in fact, miserable. There are also countless millions of folks with little or nothing, who choose to be happy, and they are in fact happy!

Regardless of the circumstances he told me, We always have that choice. Some days it will be more difficult than others, and it won't always be easy, but even if we fail, we will have a new opportunity the very next day, . .to choose to be happy.

I have never forgotten that conversation, and I have tried very hard to make that conscious choice every day, some days I didn't do well at all, but I have always tried again and guess what??? I think you all know; I have indeed been happy. I certainly can't tell anyone else how to be happy, but I can tell you that happiness will not come from riches, a big house a fancy car or job title. If you wait for someone else to make you happy, I'm afraid you will wait a very long time. It is no accident that when we "do the right thing", we feel good, we feel happy. That I believe is a universal given.

If we then choose to do the right things, aren't we in fact, "choosing to be happy". Each of you will have to sort out your own formula for happiness, but that quest begins with a simple choice each day, what kind of person do I want to be today, shall I be miserable, some days you might be perfectly justified, or despite the odds, will you choose to be happy??

I have one more thing to share with you. A man by the name of Max Erhmann wrote this in 1927. It went largely unnoticed at that time but became popular in the early 1970's and was even made into a top 40 record. Some of your parents or grandparents might remember it. Listen carefully, there is better advice here than I could ever give you.

Desiderata

**Go placidly amid the noise and the haste,
and remember what peace there may be in silence.**

**As far as possible, without surrender,
be on good terms with all persons.
Speak your truth quietly and clearly;
and listen to others,
even to the dull and the ignorant;
they too have their story.**

**Avoid loud and aggressive persons;
they are vexatious to the spirit.**

**If you compare yourself with others,
you may become vain or bitter,
for always there will be greater and lesser persons than yourself.**

**Enjoy your achievements as well as your plans.
Keep interested in your own career, however humble;
it is a real possession in the changing fortunes of time.**

Exercise caution in your business affairs,
for the world is full of trickery.
But let this not blind you to what virtue there is;
many persons strive for high ideals,
and everywhere life is full of heroism.

Be yourself. Especially do not feign affection.
Neither be cynical about love,
for in the face of all aridity and disenchantment,
it is as perennial as the grass.

Take kindly the counsel of the years,
gracefully surrendering the things of youth.

Nurture strength of spirit to shield you in sudden misfortune.
But do not distress yourself with dark imaginings.
Many fears are born of fatigue and loneliness.

Beyond a wholesome discipline,
be gentle with yourself.

You are a child of the universe
no less than the trees and the stars;
you have a right to be here.
And whether or not it is clear to you,
no doubt the universe is unfolding as it should.

Therefore be at peace with God,
whatever you conceive Him to be.
And whatever your labors and aspirations,
in the noisy confusion of life,
keep peace in your soul.

With all its sham, drudgery, and broken dreams,
it is still a beautiful world.
Be cheerful. Strive to be happy.

Max Ehrmann, Desiderata

Finally, we reach the end of our time together here at Woodstock Academy. I would wish you all good luck, but I don't think you're going to need it. I have grown close to every class that passes through here, but this one, . . .for me, . . of course, is very, very special.

I am very grateful to you for indulging me, . . for allowing me to enjoy this journey and for allowing me to be a part of it. I will indeed miss you all . .I do indeed love you all, and hope you will come back often and visit. Thank you again and remember, . . . be brave, and choose to be happy!

In many ways that speech, to my Billy's graduating class, was the precursor to this book. It sums up rather tidily the influences of those who came before me, and my delivering of it was fully intended to pass those influences on to yet another generation. The learning is never done, and I took the same, albeit a more personal approach with my younger son Daniel, and daughter Katherine, when I penned the following letters to them. I gave Daniel his, during the spring of his senior year at the Academy and when the time came to say goodbye to Katherine, daddy's girl, as we dropped her off at campus to start her college career, I gave her one as well. Each was given their letter in hopes of reminding them how very important all of this has been and should continue to be.

Daniel Letter – Senior Year

Dear Daniel,

I am VERY proud of you and all that you have accomplished. Grades close today and you currently have two A's and a B, honor roll marks in your senior year. The courses you currently have are not easy ones, maybe you think they are, but there are plenty of seniors taking basket-weaving 101 to finish the senior year, and you are not.

These are good courses that can teach you a lot, and I hope that with the hard work you are also enjoying them just a bit.

I have been telling Mom, Billy and Katherine ever since you were all very little, that "it's not as easy as you think, to be Daniel".

Being the middle child in a whole family of 'high achievers' is always a significant challenge. Remember, I was the middle child too, and I remember. There are of course a great many things that have come easily to you. Like your uncle Ricky, it seems like there just wasn't a sport you tried, that you already weren't VERY good at it, from the beginning. Lucky you!

That fact however never blinded me to all the other challenges you have faced. All of us, even your brother and sister are faced with moments of self-doubt, questioning, confusion.

This is all part of being a normal teenager finding your way in the world. Middle children however seem to have a deeper sensitivity, a more introspective, examining mind. We (middle children) worry more, we think more about 'fairness' and are less patient with what we might think is wrong, than others. It is both a blessing and a curse because if we didn't care so much, life might be easier.

I have pushed you I admit that. I have always known what GREAT potential you have, and I have seen it as my personal responsibility to do everything I can to help you achieve and succeed. It's my job, more important than anything else I do.

I want you to know how much I love you, how grateful and proud I am of your efforts. I will of course continue to be 'the dad', even a bit of a pain in the ass, but you must remember that ALL of my motivation comes from real love.

You are a fine young man. You have been given AND have earned tremendous opportunity. I believe you are on the right track. There will be temptations and mistakes that will set you back from time to time, that is true for everyone.

You have all the right stuff though, to get through it all and make a very good life for yourself.

As your senior year winds down, just remember a few guidelines. Keep your nose clean! There is still a lot at risk. All it takes is for one jealous or unhappy person to report something on you, that could make your life very difficult. Don't allow yourself to be involved or even near any nonsense that could jeopardize all that you have earned. It isn't worth the risk. This may mean you need to avoid certain situations or people down the stretch, but your truest friends will understand, any that do not, are not good friends to begin with.

I hope you continue to finish strong academically, doing so says EVERYTHING about your character. Get yourself dialed in for your final high school golf season. How far you go with it is entirely up to you. I believe, and others agree that the sky is the limit there. Your work and practice on the fairways now will build for you the confidence and ability that will make your college playing experience a good one. That is important too.

You are also in a position among your peers and especially with younger students at WA, to set a positive example. To be in a position to be admired and respected is not easy, but it is a real treasure that will only increase in value to you over time, don't take it lightly.

Keep up the good work. I TRULY am very proud of you. The work you do now, can set the tone for the life ahead of you, and the man you want to become. Yes, it's a challenge, and a big responsibility, but you know how to proceed, you know what is right and wrong and you have all the ability a young man could want. I have confidence in you, and of course I am ALWAYS here to help if I can, don't ever be afraid to ask.

I love you with all my heart and ALWAYS will.

Dad

Kat College Letter from Dad

My Dearest Katherine,

   This is a big day for sure! The first day of a whole new adventure. I am sure that you, like me, have a tangle of mixed emotions about it all. That of course is completely natural. Excitement, anxiety, enthusiasm and nerves and everything in between. I feel it all for you too, but most of all I feel incredible love and pride in my little girl.

You have been nothing but joy to me for the last 18 years. Every achievement, every effort, every smile and yes, every roll of the eyes has been a wonder for me to behold. You are an amazing young woman.

   This new transition is just another in a long line of mountains you have climbed, and I have absolute confidence in your ability to do so. If your own confidence stumbles a bit at any point, you should know that this too is completely natural, there is no achievement worth earning, that doesn't come with some trepidation.

   I have walked this journey with you, every step of the way. More often than you might think I have simply quietly observed, allowing you to chart your own course, trusting YOUR instincts and your intelligence sometimes even more than my own. I have been able to do so because over the course of your lifetime, you have earned my admiration and confidence. That has made my job a whole lot easier, and I am grateful for that.

   You have achieved so much, so many accomplishments, but you have also gracefully endured your defeats and disappointments. Life can indeed be filled with both, that is an inescapable truth. In those times of struggle, we can be consumed with worry and rendered helpless or we can simply place one foot in front of the other and take the baby steps necessary to move forward and beyond our troubles.

You have already done this more times than you may even know, and life will call upon you to do it again, more than once.

Remember this, I am always with you. I am in your head, and I put myself there on purpose, just as my father did for me. When we walk the road of life ahead of the next generation, we cannot help but learn the way. This is the natural order of things. I have walked a truly wondrous path, but it has also been filled with its share of potholes, rocks and ditches. It is every father's obligation and honor to share his experience strength and hope with his children, and mine is always at your disposal.

There is no question that cannot be asked, no fear or concern that cannot be shared, no mistake or misstep that cannot be revealed to me. I have had more than my share of my own, and I have learned from them. If and when you ever need me, I am your father and I will be there for you, and this will remain true even long after I am gone, I promise you that, I have fully intended it to be that way, from the very day you were born. If you are ever hesitant to share a concern with me, put that fear aside and trust in the fact that I am your father and that my love for you overrides everything else and ALWAYS will. When a subject is simply too uncomfortable for face to face discussion, you can always write me a note, which I will respond to in kind.

Yes, I do trust your instincts and judgment, but that does not mean that you travel alone. I am at your back, proud and comfortable with your stride and pace, but ever ready to assist you, should you stumble.

It is ok to be nervous some anxiety will make you careful, and that is a good thing. Trust yourself though, and when necessary just take one small step in the direction of your own choosing. Every long journey begins this way, with one small step, and sometimes that decision is the only one that is clear to us at the time, but every forward step taken, broadens the choices and opportunities that lie in front of us and it is the courage that compelled that first step that will keep us moving forward towards ultimate success.

Remember also that your own happiness is dependent solely upon you. If you look for others to provide it for you, I am afraid you will be sorely disappointed. Your own happiness will come easiest by way of the mirror, and an honest assessment of your own strengths and weaknesses. We all have them both, and many are afraid to look for fear of seeing the weaknesses, but in doing so, they are denying themselves the ability to truly see their own great strengths as well. We must accept both. We can pick and choose what areas of our lives are unsatisfactory and using the same one small step approach we can work on those of OUR OWN choosing, not someone else's. The very best judge of how you are doing, is YOU! Remember that, because our world often tries to impose its own standards on us, and they all too often are shallow, without real meaning to us, and frankly useless.

Maybe it all sounds very daunting, and you wonder, how can I do this by myself, . . .and the answer really is, you already have! You have already chartered your own course for years. Sure, there was some parental guidance, but going forward that guidance will be still be there both in your own head, as well as in the rules and limitations of the world you live in. You will still be making the day to day decisions and taking the small steps, as you have ALWAYS done. You need not worry, you have already won so many victories and overcome so much before, there is no reason to think you won't conquer some more.

Most of all, be brave, and CHOOSE to be happy. Regardless of the circumstances, you ALWAYS have that choice. The world is full of millionaires and people who have everything, yet they choose to focus on the negative and the result is that they are terribly unhappy. Then there are millions in our world who have virtually nothing, yet they choose to be happy, and they are, in fact, happy. Regardless of the circumstances, you ALWAYS have that choice.

I am enclosing a copy of my very favorite poem for you. I became aware of it when I was a teenager, a little younger than you are now.

It was made into a popular kind of corny song back in the day, but it has stuck with me and served as a guiding list of principles ever since. It was written about a hundred years ago by a man named Max Ehrman. Keep a copy of it and refer back to it from time to time. I think it is remarkable and provides beautiful witness to how we might best conduct our lives. I could not possibly love you any more than I do. Remember I am always with you.

With all my love,

    Dad

With the children safely embarked on their own paths and seemingly as best prepared as we were able to make them, my wife decided that she too, needed to pursue a path of her own. This was of course a very difficult revelation for me, as it was no doubt for her as well. Despite my misgivings about her decision, I resigned myself to the reality of it. If I did not, what kind of hypocritical message would I be sending to our children. I had spent a lifetime telling them that only they could decide what was best for them. How could that not also be true for their mother? So, we parted ways, fairly amicably I am happy to say. At some point in the process, it occurred to me, that yes this too, was just one more opportunity for real and meaningful learning.

<u>Divorce day</u>

Today was a big day for me, . . not the very best of days, but certainly an important one. It marks the culmination of an extended period of significant personal challenge, not the first in my life, and undoubtably not the last. During the course of this period I have tried to focus first and foremost on adhering to the principles I was raised on. It is interesting to note, that the older I get, the more important those things taught to me as a boy, have become.

Tomorrow I will wake up on the other side, and as my friend Scotty says, "begin my newest chapter".

Over the course of the day today, there were lots of i's to dot and t's to cross and I spent a good deal of time out and about completing my necessary tasks. On my way home this afternoon, after seeing a good number of people I run into out here in my Quiet Corner of Connecticut, the thought occurred to me, once again, how much I love this community and the many, many friends I have made out here over the last 25 years.

In the course of daily living, if you can go about your business and continuously run into smiling faces, warm regards, and generally good and decent folks, then indeed you are blessed. This has been my good fortune and I know also that it is not limited to those that I see on a regular basis.

Tonight when I lay my head again on my pillow and thank God for all the many blessings he has bestowed upon me, too numerous to even count anymore, . . I will take note especially of all the kind, compassionate and really terrific people he has sent into my life, they too, are too numerous to count. They count in my heart though, and I am VERY grateful for all of them.

Tomorrow is another day, the journey continues and I remain the same fellow I was yesterday, a little older and grayer, maybe a bit wiser, but ultimately the same little red headed, freckled face boy I was a hundred years ago, still full of marvel and wonder at all of life's little blessings, and eternally grateful for all of them.

"It's a Hard Life Wherever You Go"

A wise man once said, . . "it's a hard life, wherever you go", . . . That wise man, was my own mentor and older brother Rick, upon whom I have relied for such wisdom for all of my days!

The phrase is true enough for all of us I suppose. We all have our struggles and even the most comfortable of lives are fraught with bumps in the road. This is the human condition, the world we live in can seem dark and foreboding and we all face periods of uncertainty, trial and torment.

Having said that, and understanding the truth of it, I for one, will not yield. I will never surrender my peace or solace to a hostile world around me.

On the contrary, . . .I will combat the darkness, yes even with a hint of arrogant defiance, I will live the best life I can and sleep ever so soundly at night knowing I have done so.

When faced with the sometimes-cruel realities of everyday life, I often think of a couple of lines from my favorite poem, Desiderata;

"Nurture strength of spirit to shield you in sudden misfortune. But do not distress yourself with dark imaginings. Many fears are born of fatigue and loneliness."

And

"But let this not blind you to what virtue there is; many persons strive for high ideals, and everywhere life is full of heroism."

I will continue to pursue the joy, and the light that is offered in every day, too often overlooked or ignored, but ever-present in ALL of our lives if we will only seek it out.

I will stare down life's dark storms, plodding on through the pouring rain until the clouds surrender to me, and the very wind of my stride blows them afar from the shining sun.

I am resolute in my pursuit. That is who I am, and who I was meant to be.

Having come all this way, through all of the joys and sorrows, the trials and tribulations, and the wonder and worry, I find myself contented with a life well lived. I will be 60 years old in a little over a month. Still very young for having lived such a full life. Although two of the children remain at home with me, they are very busy creating their own road. I very much enjoy quietly watching them do so, albeit it from a safe and non-intrusive distance. I have complete confidence in all three of them. Already I can see how much further down the road to happiness and success they are, than I was at their age. What father would not be pleased by such a fact? So, I am left now to my own devices.

I know this much; I am not at all done living, or loving. I think that, more than anything else, it is my mission on this little blue ball. That loving will not be limited to other's either. I will work to extend it to them of course, but I aim also to be sure to include myself. I think I have earned it, and as a very dear friend recently told me, 'it's my turn now'.

60-year-old gentleman

What is it do you suppose, that a 60 year old single gentleman looks for in a relationship.

I am 60, I am single after being married for 25 years, I aim to be a gentleman, and I think I know!

A man at my age is a far cry from a twenty-five-year-old, that is for certain. At the age of 60 we are faced pretty seriously with our own mortality. Couple this with a lifetime of loving and learning and an entirely new perspective is inevitable.

A man of 60 is no longer tethered to the demands of building a career, nor is he carrying the weight of responsibility of providing for and safeguarding his family. If he is worth his salt, he has labored diligently for many years in both of those endeavors, and the respite is welcome. That's not to say he did not enjoy those efforts, but I do think our modern world seriously underestimates the level of commitment and energy that they require. A lot of good men at 60, are frankly, just a little tired.

A man of 60, with a brain in his head, will seek out only the very best in a relationship partner. He will look for someone strong, smart, capable and independent. He will do this in no small part, because he himself has had to be these things for a very long time, he knows the value of them, and through his efforts, has sincerely come to appreciate them for what they are.

An added benefit of finding such a woman, will be that she will innately understand who he is, what he has accomplished, and what it took for him to do so. He will, in her eyes, be valued for those very things that mean so much to him.

A gentleman of 60, like any man, has probably seen his share of superficial dalliances. Our modern 'hook-up' culture is replete with them and any man who grew up in these times has experienced this, denial of such is just nonsense. However, the gentleman put those things behind him long, long ago. The life he has led, has required commitment, teamwork, compromise, tolerance, patience and most of all perseverance. Things such as conquest, competition, gamesmanship, and scorekeeping, though often present in his 'working world', have long vanished from the world of his heart and soul, they just don't fit there anymore. He has no time for them, nor inclination to indulge in them.

The 60-year-old gentleman wants a partner, a loving companion, a helper and supporter, **an ear and mind for things of significance***, and a true friend.*

He will look for someone HE can learn with, and from.

Sadly, our culture has often robbed men of equal opportunity in love. That may not make immediate sense to many, but I believe that it is often the case.

Men are required to focus on too many other things, and genuine love unfortunately often falls down lower on the priority list. It is not that men don't want it or know how to exercise it. They simply do not have the time, or energy left to devote to it.

The 60-year-old man now has that time, and again, if he has a brain in his head, his priorities have indeed shifted dramatically.

I do envy those rare couples who survive it all and are able to reach this point together. They will be poised to provide such great comfort and joy to each other in these quieter years, AND they will have the time to do so. We all know who they are, we see them all the time. Older couples who obviously adore just being next to each other. What a great achievement, and what a fitting reward for their efforts.

The 60 year old gentleman will notice them every time, and he will hope against all odds, . . . that he might still find it in a woman his own age, who has endured as much, survived as much, and deserves and will appreciate it as much, as he does.

Chapter eight:
Love and Romance

Life without love and romance, isn't really living at all. It all began at five years old with my making googly eyes at little Judy from school, the one with the big bright eyes and an even brighter smile!

I couldn't wait to see her every day at school and searched for her every single Sunday at church. Somehow, just seeing her was enough.

She and I have maintained a very special friendship from six to sixty, and that is a treasure that simply cannot be overstated. There were so many St Mary sweethearts. She was the first of many, and I have lost count of how many others after all the years. I haven't really forgotten them though, from that sweet girl at church through to the end of my time there in 6th grade and the feisty and lovely blonde in 'Swiss Miss' braids riding home on the same bus with me each day wearing the school's newly designed plaid jumper. I fondly remember them all, and most importantly, how they made me feel. Then continuing on to the broken heart in my teen years when circumstances separated me from not one, but two loves of my life, back to back. Terribly heart-wrenching and seismic events, that affected every relationship I ever had thereafter. All the way to my current appreciation for the women I have watched age with stunning grace and beauty that defies all conventional thinking. I have been caught in a whirlwind of romance for my entire life! It all began with my beloved grandmother Molly, who when I was a very young boy was convinced that I would grow up to be a priest! At the same time however, she would insist "Charlie dear, tell me about ALL of your girlfriends", and implore me to read to her from a book of romantic poetry. Molly should have known then, that this little 'Divel', as she would call me in her Irish brogue, would never get to the seminary, despite my nearly flawless imitation of the entire mass on Sundays, in her living room for her tea party guests. Don't think for a moment that I did not notice the genuine affection from those little old ladies either. I was set on a course that would render me weak in the knees for the fairer sex, for all of my days to come. The following poems and tomes are a chronicle of that obsession, and the true and raw emotion that afflicts more men than will admit it, or that many might imagine. They however, not having been blessed with my Molly, or the Irish gift of gab, spend most of their lives with thoughts like these hidden way deep down inside. I am happy to release them, for them.

Autumn in New England holds a special magic for me, and always has. Even as a boy, the return to school brought wonder and adventure to mind. Many years later, with some more mature wonders under my belt, I penned the following poem in tribute to all those autumns and the lovely sentiments they brought with them, and to a lovely young lady from my past, with fire in her spirit and a 'divel' of her own in her mischievous smile.

Autumn Air

Warm sun, cool breeze

Autumn air, golden leaves.

Spinning, twirling, floating down

Piling gently,

on cool damp ground.

Reds and golds, greens and brown,

The quiet of morn, the little sounds.

Memory stirs, like rustling leaves,

Old Octobers, the mind's eye sees.

Warming heart, warming rays,

Cool clear eyes, from yesterdays.

Cooling breeze, falling leaves,

Warm sweet smile, the mind's eye sees.

Yellow leaves and golden hair,

Treasured thoughts from yesteryear.

Crimson cheeks and wrinkled nose,

Autumn strikes a lovely pose.

My mind's eye sees and can't forget,

Those autumn days when we first met.

Warm sun, cool breeze,

Autumn air, golden leaves.

Each year, I spend some time,

Letting autumns old, fill my mind.

Spinning, twirling, leaves of gold,

Warm, rich thoughts, of days of old.

Years gone by, autumns past,

Thoughts of you that always last.

I have been blessed with loves I simply cannot justify, and in recognition of that fact, I can only admit the truth and power those loves have cast over me. The following speaks to that quiet place within that only the truest of love can reach and the girl that once, and perhaps always will, take me there.

<u>Eyes of Love</u>

There is a place so deep within,

Way deep down inside.

That quiet place far away,

is where my heart, my soul reside.

No one goes there, no one can.

A tender place, it can't be touched.

There resides both boy and man,

and there is where I feel too much.

A lonely place, that place within,

even I don't go, my visits rare.

It's not a place to let others in,

My heart and soul laid out bare.

Your eyes go there

How is that so?

And when you look

What do they know?

What do they see

When you visit there?

My heart and soul,

laid out bare?

And how do you find the way

The path so straight,

It's from your eyes, right to that gate.

This is how it's always been

And yet somehow, I still don't know.

How is it so your searing gaze,

Exactly knows which way to go?

I hope someday you'll take me there,

for that's a place I seldom go.

I'll go with you, without the fear,

Your eyes of love, the way, they know.

Although my grandmother Molly surely introduced me to the concept of romantic love, it was these young women who clarified and demonstrated its real and lasting power. A power I remain helpless in the face of, and for the record, happily so.

Each, in their own way, made crucial and permanent impressions on my heart, and each remains the lien holder on portions thereof.

Yes, it is a bit crowded in there, . . . such is the burden of this wealthy landlord of love's most beautiful tenements.

What exactly is, . . .real love?

A timeless and loaded question ask a hundred people and you will get a hundred different answers. Our innate need to love, and be loved, may very well be our most powerful natural instinct. Witness the child who clings to and endures a relationship with an abusive parent. The need to love and be loved can over-ride seemingly illogical circumstances.

Our modern culture has horribly distorted what true love really is, to the point where often we fail to recognize that which we need so very much, and we then exercise futile effort to gain the false comfort of unfulfilling and very poor substitutes.

Real love, and the true happiness we derive from it, does not come from the superficial and brief pleasures that come from money, sex or power. It is not the comfort that we gain from a lack of conflict or difficulty in our lives, or the temporary distraction obtained when we are 'entertained' or showered with praise or adoration. It does not suffer disappointment or from mistakes we all can make, it sets no expectation or mandate, . . .it simply is.

Real love is a state of complete fulfillment brought about most often through self-sacrifice, self-awareness and the honest and UNCONDITIONAL caring we can offer another. When we genuinely act in the interest of true love, the positive result and ensuing happiness is experienced not solely by the object of our affection, but also by ourselves. We know best, when we have loved most purely.

We feel it every bit as much, and perhaps even more so, than the person to whom we have extended that love.

Real love is completely unconditional, it requires no reciprocation because its very existence and practice already answers that call.

The human capacity for love is really quite astounding, yet in our modern confusion about what it really is, we too often stumble around in the dark, chasing empty substitutes and feeling ultimately alone and unloved. The old Beatles song, . . .'All you need is love', is true, but sadly for too many, love has become almost impossible to recognize and thus partake in.

We, as a species, are designed to love, and be loved. It is in that endeavor that we find true happiness and fulfillment. That happiness is not contingent upon whether we are loved, but rather that we do love, unconditionally. That is the ultimate fulfillment of purpose and satisfaction in our lives. Through that pursuit we gain a sense of peace and contentment not attainable through any other means. That 'happiness' is not diminished by hardship or difficulty; in fact it is often enhanced by it. A dear and gentle love once told me, . . . "the energy that love creates, cannot be destroyed", and I believe her to this day.

When we find and experience true love, nothing in this world can shake it, or diminish it.

The older I get, the more I realize that this is our reason for being. To love unconditionally, as best we can, given our multitude of human frailties and weaknesses.

The road to this 'nirvana', is fraught with hazards and risks, but given a taste of what true love really is, only a complete fool would not embark on a path that seeks it, It is our reason for living. Make no mistake though, finding true love and happiness is not a destination, not an end point to the journey, but rather, it is the road map, the 'GPS' that we are meant to follow. The destinations will come and go, but as my mother wisely told me, "the real joy, will be in the journey"!

The lure of the ocean and of our hearts seem inextricably tied together. Perhaps this too is an Irish thing, or simply innate in any people who spend lives close to the sea. Is there anyone, on any dating app, who does not profess to enjoy the time honored ideal of 'walks on the beach'? I for one cannot deny it, something in that salt air and cool wet sand just does it for me, and I know full well I am not alone in that feeling. Our best dates, and most memorable moments of romance and overwhelming affection so very often occur by the water. Even if our reality does not include such iconic imagery, the picture we paint in our imaginations very often does. Hollywood and the greeting card folks certainly understand this and take full advantage of it in selling us the idyllic wonder of anything from toothpaste to automobiles, on salty aired, sandy shores.

I wrote the following poem about a girl I never actually went to the beach with. it doesn't matter that we never got to the shore, because in my heart, that's where we always were.

Seaside Sunset

Sunset glows through salty mist,
coral hues light rolling waves.
Blushing cheeks, by cool air kissed,
memories kept the mind's eye saves.

Harping gulls sing day is done.
Naked toes splash the tidal zone.
Walk with me, in the setting sun.
The moment ours, ours alone.

My mind's eye walks along this shore.
My heart fuels thoughts of days of yore.
Loving eyes, misty glean,
loving smile, the mind's eye dreams.

Whispered breath, speaks with those eyes.
Simple words, those eyes can't lie.
Tender fingers in my hand,
electric touch to reach my soul.

A cool breeze and wet sand,

love's embrace, against the cold.

That evening air, the breeze of the sea,

brings all these thoughts, alive in me.

We stand alone on cool damp sand.

parting now, with tear filled eyes.

Fingers touch, a trembling hand,

The time has come to say goodbyes.

Smiling sad, the mind's dream ends.

Aching hearts,

the dream helps mend.

Beauty lies in those seaside eyes,

and a lingering kiss, . . .

'ere we say goodbye.

Taken altogether, beginning as a young boy seeking his beloved grandmother's approval and love, through all of the twists and turns, laboring and learning that a life of loves can bring, I have come to see it all as THE most vital component of our lives, or at least mine anyway, and I have no reservation in that assertion.

"Love of Love, Love of Life, and giving without measure" *

* from the song "The Dream", by the Moody Blues

If there is one thing that the sum total of my own life experience has taught me, it is that far too many of us go through life completely missing the point of it all.

Again, Like young Emily asks, in the wonderful Thornton Wilder play, Our Town, . . "Do any human beings ever realize life while they live it, every, every minute?"

"No", replies the stage manager, "the saints, and poets, maybe, ... they do some."

We have been told time and time again by all of history's greatest thinkers, and yes, by the 'Saints and Poets' too, that the key to life in this often cold hard world, . . is Love.

Jesus Christ, the greatest of them all, instructed us that LOVE was what we are, or should be all about.

I'm afraid very few of us really ever understand it though. As a species we are saddled with a good number of handicaps that consistently get in the way of our understanding.

There is a constant battle, from the day we are born, between our innate, animal nature and instincts, and our souls. Our souls it seems to me, were created of stuff not of this world, from a higher plane. Our souls do not survive or thrive on the things of this earth, on food or even water, but of things of an almost incomprehensible nature. Things of heaven, and thus, beyond our full understanding.

We are indeed an intelligent species, and as such, we certainly can grasp the concept of love, and of our own need for it, both giving and receiving. Our trouble comes when we try to incorporate it into our earth-based existence. All of those animal, and natural, instincts, then get in the way. Somehow, this is at the root, of what the bible calls, our 'Fallen nature'.

The closest we come to a full understanding is when we try to fathom the concept of 'unconditional love'. It's ironic that so many are only able to exercise this with pets, because they require so little of us, and do not seem to be saddled with the same selfish interests that come with the 'human' package.

So many of us spend virtually all of our lives chasing a form of love that suits us first, that conforms to our own wants and needs, and when we cannot find it, (as is too often the case), we grow embittered and even skeptical of its very existence. Then we join much of the rest of the world in saying the words, playing the game, but never really loving anyone at all, not even ourselves.

In the bible in Corinthians we read;

"Love is patient, love is kind. It does not envy, it does not boast, it is not proud. It is not rude, it is not self-seeking, it is not easily angered, it keeps no record of wrongs. Love does not delight in evil but rejoices with truth. It always protects, always trusts, always hopes and ALWAYS perseveres."

Read it again slowly, . . . how few understand this?

Nearly all of us begin our lives in this world as recipients of this very same love. As infants, our loving parents have no qualms with our foibles, or imperfections, on the contrary they are often recognized as uniquely our own and thus things mom and dad simply love about us.

Our love returned to them is equally unconditional, the infant isn't put off my mommy's bad breath, or the hair in daddy's nose, they are part and parcel of the love the child feels coming from that parent, and exuberantly accepted as such.

Somewhere along the way, for many, this state of mutually unconditional and purest of love fades, and is replaced by a pseudo-love, defined by a world built by flawed men and women. In our hubris and human arrogance, we crudely attempt to redefine that love, in a way that best suits our own worldview.

And we never bother to look back, to review and compare what we have given up on.

As we grow and age, our minds become increasing cluttered with all of history's and mankind's errors in understanding. Let's face it, they far outnumber our wisdom and achievements.

The speed and volume of our current world only makes the problem worse, as we are bombarded with falsehoods, mixed messaging, deception and all of the other human failings on a constant basis.

It is no wonder at all that we are so confused and lost.

Love really is, all you need. Sadly though, we have almost completely forgotten what love is, what it really is.

The next time you tell someone "I love you', take just a moment and ask yourself what that really means. I think that is a healthy and helpful exercise, and if we do it often enough, we might just begin to really remember, what it is we are actually saying.

In concluding this chapter, consider a lifetime of learning and loving, and the maturation that inevitably occurs. Wouldn't we all be blessed if we could confidently assert that we had truly enjoyed this lifetime as a Labor of Love.

<u>Labored in Love</u>

I've labored in love these many long years.
My wages were paid in both smiles and in tears.

I've traveled through time,
to pause and reflect
in the quiet of dusk
or the dawn of new days.

I've labored in love,
for that's been my trade.
Full wages were paid,
a full life has been made.

My journey's my own, though many have joined.
My labor of love, a life of its own.

Will anyone know, will my story live on?

I'll pause and reflect,
and renew each year.
my story goes on with new hope,
and new fear.

I'll labor in love for a few more years.
For I have wages to earn,
in both smiles and in tears.

Chapter Nine:
Gratitude

In the 1960's my parents were heavily involved in a movement of spiritual renewal within the Catholic church called 'Cursillo'. The movement began in Spain in 1944. The concept is defined on their web page as follows:

"Cursillos in Christianity is a movement within the church that, through a method of its own tries to, and through God's grace manages to; enable the essential realities of the Christian to come to life in the uniqueness, originality, and creativity of each person. In becoming aware of their potential and while accepting their limitations they exercise their freedom by their conviction, strengthen their will with their decision, to propitiate friendship in virtue of their constancy in both their personal and community life.

The Cursillo Movement consists of proclaiming the best news of the best reality: that God, in Christ, loves us. Communicated by the best means, which is friendship towards the best of each one, which is his being person and his capacity of Conviction, Decision, and Constancy."

These ideas, as well as those fostered within my Dad and Mom by their own lives and experiences, were the guideposts within which our entire family was nurtured. Our kitchen on Anchorage road was always bedecked with small posters proclaiming "Decolores" which is Spanish for 'in colors'.

This one word carried great import in our little world because the meaning behind it for those involved with the Cursillo movement was a lot more than just colors. It is perhaps best defined on a web page from the Cursillo Movement of Canada, of which my parents were among the principle founders. It is stated there as follows;

"If there are sad moments in life, there are also others when we see everything in color. This is the case of a person who discovers that he or she is loved by the very person that he or she loves! For lovers, everyday life loses its sadness, the sun shines, life is beautiful, and we see it through rose-colored spectacles."

I have, on more than one occasion been accused of that very same approach, of seeing life through rose colored glasses. So be it, for this is who I was taught to be. Perhaps what I recall most vividly about my parent's involvement in what was at the time a rather controversial approach to Catholicism, was the concept of Palanca, or sacrifice offered for the benefit of others. It was a bedrock practice within the movement, and in our home at Anchorage road as well.

Palanca

One of the most valuable lessons of my youth, from my parents, was the introduction to the Catholic concept of 'Palanca'.

Palanca is a Spanish word that means 'lever'. Think of using a lever to lift a load you might not normally be able to,. .A 'palanca letter' gives support and guidance in the form of a prayer, sacrifice and honest communication, written and offered to a loved one, family member or stranger who might be facing struggle or embarking on a new venture.

My parents were very active members and participants in a Catholic spiritual renewal movement called 'Cursillo' in the 60's, Palanca was an important component of that movement and can be described in the following manner;

"prayers and sacrifices ...[to provide] help to overcome the resistance to grace for those for whom we pray."

As children, we were encouraged to write 'Palanca letters' to friends and family members who were either embarking on new challenges or facing some form of difficulty. The idea was for us to first, gain empathy and understanding of the other's situation, and then to offer up sacrifices, labors and prayers in solidarity and support for them.

When my three older brothers went to Guatemala as teenagers to witness first-hand the distribution of charitable funds that they had raised for Oxfam through the now famous 'Franklin hunger walk', of which they were principle founders and organizers, we younger siblings all wrote them 'letters of Palanca' in support of their mission.

What 'Palanca' taught us all, was to be ever mindful of both the trials and tribulations of others, AND of our own blessings and good fortune. To face life's challenges and the crosses we all bear armed with the strength and armor provided by a real appreciation for all the gifts that we had in fact been given. In a world consumed by 'me first', instant gratification, and a myriad of other vices that cloud our natural abilities of compassion, generosity and kindness, . . . the idea of self-sacrifice, of putting others needs and concerns first, . . of 'Palanca' as it were, seems to me, to be worth revisiting. It has proven, for me at least, to be among my own life's greatest gifts.

In my youth, I wrote many of those 'Palanca' letters, and I distinctly remember the good feelings that were always generated within when I did. It is certainly possible that along with my grandmother's romantic impulses, my father's English teaching, and my own propensity to 'gab', the practice of writing down sincere and meaningful thoughts and ideas, had its origins in those letters. My brother David and I wrote letters to each other many times during the one year in our education that we were apart.

He had earned a soccer scholarship at Southern Connecticut State, and I had not yet committed to further schooling in our first year out of high school.

A year later Dave would transfer to the University of Massachusetts in Amherst, and I would join him there, back together where we belonged. I also wrote volumes of letters to my many sweethearts, let's just face it, I was a pretty good letter writer. There were however many letters I did not write, for a wide variety of reasons, that looking back now, I wish I had. The following, which I obviously have now written, is one of them and a good example of what a continuing practice of honest introspection can offer;

A letter of thanks, 45 years later

Dear Bill,

It has been my good fortune during this most unfortunate time of Covid and national disruption, to have been granted plenty of excess time on my hands. This has afforded me the opportunity to wax philosophically, to ponder a great many things, and to write, something I very much enjoy doing. Alas,. . the silver lining, I suppose.

As a 60-year-old man who has successfully raised three wonderful children, I have gained a perspective that I do believe, you will appreciate.

There is of course, particular irony in that, enough to cause a grin, and at least on my part, a healthy dose of humility.

You see, I can clearly see the world around me from eyes like yours that gazed across a dining room table at me, back in Franklin Mass, seemingly a hundred years ago!

I have two sons, and a beautiful 20-year-old daughter, and they have been nothing short of my raison d'etre.

Almost fifty years ago, when I saw you last, you were the fellow who spirited away my heart, my love. Like any young man would be, I was both devastated, and angry. How could you do such a thing to either of us, especially to 'my girl'.

I know now, how off the mark my young thinking was. She wasn't 'my girl' at all, she was still very much YOUR girl, and a very lucky girl to boot!

For the record, I didn't 'hate' you, to my credit I was too smart for that. Resentful, yes, hateful, no.

I find it both gratifying and incredibly ironic that I eventually grew into the type of man, that would look awful familiar to you. I have been a stalwart defender of all of my children. A gentle, but firm and resolute leader of 'Seal team Harrington', as it were. I also know full well, the difference that has made for them, and for me.

Perhaps a letter like this is long overdue, I'm not so sure though, because a lot of learning has been required prior to its composition. I will say this, I am very comfortable now, with my admiration for you. Your daughter is a beautiful woman, and you and EJ did a remarkable job with her. I know for certain that she adores you, and now, as a father of similar stripes, I understand why, very clearly.

It's never too late to be grateful, so I will thank you.

I thank you specifically for your example, for your dedication to your family, a lifetime of hard work, and for your service to our nation as well.

I have been working my whole life, to be the kind of man you have been, and without the examples I have had in my life, I never would have known what to shoot for.

May God continue to bless you, EJ, and your children.

Contemplation – Gratitude

Next to courage, perhaps the human trait I believe to be most important and valuable is gratitude.

We live in a world where so very much is taken for granted, and woefully unappreciated.

Growing up in the middle of nine wild urchins in far less than ideal financial circumstances taught me some very valuable lessons, among these, the willingness to stand apart from the crowd (Courage), and the ability to discern the real value of people and things in my life that are blessings, (Gratitude).

My father had a golden rule at our house, . . ." Don't measure". It seems that in our world today it is all about the measuring. Who has the most toys? Who has the most rights? Even Who has the most burdens? The focus is all wrong. A step back from it all provides proper perspective.

We all have cell phones, (some of us even new fancy 'smart-phones finally!), we all have big widescreens, too many cars, food on our tables, and a multitude of social media 'friends'.

Yet still, we whine and complain about what someone else has, or what we do not, or worse, we resent others good fortune because we foolishly 'measure' against our own twisted sense of entitlement.

Most importantly we have people in our lives that work and sacrifice to make our own way easier, others who put our interests first before their own. So many fail to recognize this, so caught up in the race for their own measuring, they fail to see how much is given to them each and every day.

Growing up the way I did taught me to treasure not so much things, but people. There are so many people that have contributed to my well-being, I remember them all, and think of them often.

Our age of instant communication, text messaging and digital everything is replacing human interaction, desensitizing us to the real treasure of interpersonal discourse and relationship. We fail to notice the real people in our worlds and focus instead on the fantasy provided in a digital world outside of reality, no responsibility, no requirements, no commitments and no gratitude! We take it all for granted, and we are fools for doing so.

An 'attitude of gratitude' goes a very long way.

Look around and seek out those who participate in your world in a positive way,. . and thank them! Not simply with words, but with action, be the person someone else thinks of as 'a blessing'. Try to make someone's day a little easier, a little more joyful. Most importantly, rather than focusing on all that you don't have, or all that you have to do, think for just a minute about all that has or is being done for you, in little ways, every single day. A true accounting may be surprising!

Way back at the start of this adventure, on the dedication page, and throughout the book, I have mentioned the great Thornton Wilder play, "Our Town". My participation in that production in February of 2020, was something I will never forget. It obviously was not simply the adventure of acting or working with so many great kids and the adults as well, all of which I enjoyed enormously. It was far more than that. The role of the Stage Manager, so seemingly written just for me by Mr. Wilder, and my friend Rich Telford's absolute insistence that I take it on, came at exactly the right time. Isn't it funny how those things work?

The character of the stage manager himself, the profound message of the play and the circumstances of my participation all had a great deal to do with the writing of this book. I should say correctly, in the 'compiling' of this book. After all, I have been writing it now, for just shy of sixty years.

Perhaps my favorite scene from the play comes during the third act in the cemetery. The Stage Manager, speaking directly to the audience and referring to the 'dead' sitting in the cemetery behind him says;

"**Now, there may be some things they're gonna say here that, well, might hurt your feelings some. …. But that's just the way it is. Mother and daughter, husband and wife, enemy and enemy, money or miser, all those terribly important things kind of grow pale around here, …. and what's left when your memory is gone, and your identity, … Mrs. Smith.**"

This comes amidst a long monologue addressed to the audience wherein the character outlines the idea that **"there is something eternal, about every human being"**.

Our memories and memories of us, in the end really are all we have left. They represent the sum of our existence, the record of our lives and learning, and the lessons we can leave behind. In this book I have tried to do exactly that. The lessons of my own life are intrinsically entwined with an enormous list of little memories and occurrences. Together they weave a tale that I suspect might be quite similar to that of many others of my time. Those similarities perhaps lie less in the specific details, but rather in the emotion, effect and meanings of the memories.

Not all of the memories are pleasant ones, but not all are tragic either. Taken as a whole, as an honest telling of the tale, they do tell a wonderful story. To the many friends over the years who so often asked, "Charlie, when are you going to write a book?"

Here is your answer, but you all know every bit as well as I do, we have all been writing our own books for all of our lives. It is just not everyone of us that have, as Lillian LaRosa so aptly stated, those many, many years ago, the Irish 'gift of gab'.

Since I was a very young boy, the one thing I wanted to be more than anything else was a 'dad'.

How many men can confidently say at 60, that they have achieved their life's greatest goal?

Epilogue – The Plan

My dear old dad was right to provide me with the armor he instinctively knew I would need. That armor has protected and served me so very well over all of these years. In his efforts to protect me, he taught me to protect myself using whatever abilities I could muster to do so. It worked! I have, like many others, weathered these years, through all of the storms and turbulence. What is even better, is the armor I was provided enabled me to not only survive, but to stand far taller than my five feet 6 inches, and to truly be my mother's 'Giant in a little body'.

As I get older and things slow down enough to spend some quality time just thinking, ... I grow more convinced that there may in fact be a plan, after all.

None of us knows what the heck is going on half the time, and if we are not too damn busy to figure it out, then we simply cannot see the forest for the trees, as the old expression says.

Given quiet time to 'contemplate' however, I can't help but wonder about all the whys and wherefores, and then I find myself slowly arriving at the conclusion that it really is all part of 'the plan'.

That does not mean I have figured out the rest of the plan, or even tomorrow's portion of it.

What it does do though, is provide strength, comfort and solace. Yes, things apparently do happen for reasons, reasons well above our paygrade as mere mortals, but reasons none the less.

My own private belief, that I will share here, is that once we are done and move on from this world, it all becomes crystal clear. There will be no more questions, no more doubts, and even no more regrets. There will only be truth, complete comprehension, and peace. I do believe that.

That is my faith, instilled in me by my loving parents, proven over a lifetime, and it has sustained and strengthened me for all of my days.

I think as we get older, life's circumstances start to accumulate enough evidence to convince us of that possibility. It all at least, starts to make a little sense.

With age does come wisdom, sometimes hard earned, but in the end, so very worth it.

My mother spent a good many years wailing in distress over the unfairness of life. It was only at the end, in her final few years, that she changed the title of her own story from "A journey of pain" to "A journey of Love", and God Bless her, she was good enough to admit that to me so that I might alter my own perspective a bit earlier than she did.

I think maybe I am just beginning to fully resign myself to the plan, . . . and I also think that is a very good thing. History has proven to me, that 'the plan' can be trusted, ... that it was designed by capable management much higher up the ladder than I.

I trust the plan, and am going to try to go with it, as best I can. Doing so just might provide me with the very best in the years to come. Shame I didn't start figuring this out a little sooner I suppose, but better late than never!

Give it a try, trust the plan.

And, . . as dear old dad often said, .

. ."Be brave, CHOOSE to be happy!"